WHEN SHALL THESE THINGSBE?

Old Testament Prophecy and the Revelation of John

A BASIC GUIDE TO UNDERSTANDING

Edward A. Thomas

Published by Zaccmedia
www.zaccmedia.com
info@zaccmedia.com

Published October 2015

ISBN: 978-1-909824-96-6

British Library Cataloguing-in-Publication Data
A catalogue record for this book is available from the British Library.

Cover photograph by Edward Thomas: Ein Gedi – Water from the rock.

CONTENTS

CONTENTS

ACKNOWLEDGEMENTS

Without the thorough and scholarly work of William E. Biederwolf (1867–1939), this book would not have been possible. I am grateful to him and to the person who, many years ago, gave me a copy of his book, *The Prophecy Handbook.* This has proved to be an invaluable guide into all the areas of prophecy that I have studied over the years.

I am also grateful for the study material and advice I have received from Dr Arnold G. Fruchtenbaum, Th.M., Ph.D., the founder of Ariel Ministries. His teaching came to my notice when, many years ago, I heard him speak and first discovered an interest in Israel, a subject never taught in any detail, if at all, in any church I had attended. As part of my growing awareness of the purposes of God regarding that much maligned nation I also owe much to the teachings of Dr David L. Cooper, from whom I have gained additional understanding.

I am very much indebted to Dr Don Hender, B.Th., D.Th., Ph.D., D.Litt., of Prophetic Witness Movement International, for his willingness to read the manuscript, bring suggestions and advice, and for his encouraging endorsement.

I'm also grateful to Kath Turner for her patient and meticulous work in reading and correcting the draft manuscript of this book.

My thanks go to Paul Stanier for his very positive help in getting this book published.

Last but not least I give thanks to the Lord for my wife, Joan. For many years she has stood alongside me to support and encourage through times both of joy and sadness, success and disappointment.

PREFACE

I have chosen to use the Hebrew name Yeshua in this study when referring to our Lord rather than the English derivation of the Greek. The exceptions will be when quoting directly from the Bible text.

FOREWORD

The study of prophecy has suffered much at the hands of those who may have genuinely sought to discern the truth who, probably unwittingly, have succeeded in distorting the truth. The consequence has been that there have been those who have sought to assign to the Scriptures far more than was intended while others avoid assigning any real meaning at all to the prophecies themselves. It is generally acknowledged that little time has been given by preachers and teachers to addressing prophecy particularly in regard to the 'end times' and to the return of the Lord Yeshua. This book has been written in an attempt to bring a true balance to help the real seekers after truth and is not intended to be used for mere cursory reading. The hope is that it will assist all those who desire to study the Scriptures and to understand what they really do say.

So, is there anything of value to be learned through studying the Book of Revelation? There are many diverse elements of theology that develop different perspectives, some negative, some realistic, and others revealing vivid imaginations. One popular element, for instance, says that the symbolism the Book contains is too vague and obscure to be of any value; it is therefore impossible to understand it. If anyone does read it, it can only be seen as describing a battle between good and evil, between God and Satan, with good winning out in the end. At the other end of the spectrum there is the view that takes the symbolism as the basis for sensationalism, wild speculation and a good deal of colourful imagination, the results of which can be fantasy going beyond the realms of science fiction. All these views, and there are many others in between, have done a great deal of damage to the Book and to the fascinating truths it contains.

If we consider all these views, is there any value at all in our studying this Book? Does it make any contribution to our understanding of God's purposes for mankind, and particularly for Israel? The answer to both these questions is an emphatic yes, for in the first twenty chapters we have an inclusive collection, in chronological order, of the contents of Old Testament prophecy, containing as it does more than 500 references, even if there are no direct quotations. It is only in the two final chapters that there is any really new material. We shall find the symbolism contained in this Book is the same as that used throughout the Old Testament, the Jewish *Tanakh*, where it reveals the vital importance of the consistency of scripture, but sheer volume makes it impossible to itemise each and every case of this. However, taking just one example, we find in Revelation 1:20 the seven angels of the seven churches are described as stars, where the usage of the word 'stars' is invariably meaning angels as has been established in the Old Testament.

The title of this book, *When Shall These Things Be?*, expresses the question that is in many people's minds today as they view the situations in the world, the breakdown of morality, the wars and violence, and the many natural disasters. Many of the questions reveal a deep-seated fear and anxiety, but they also display a sad lack of knowledge of what is God's intent. We need to understand that there is a purpose behind all that is happening and is yet to happen. Using the twin pillars of reason and logic, and a bit of common sense, to support the thoughts I have expressed, coupled with simple language for easy reading, I trust the readers of this book will find answers to their questions and know the security that underlines its content – that God is the Supreme Being of the universe and is in total control of all future events, however hard and difficult they may prove to be.

This book is intended as an impartial study from the perspective of simple exegesis of the appropriate parts of the Old and New Testaments that reveal the future glorious appearing of our Lord and Saviour, Yeshua HaMaschiach (Jesus the Messiah). It has been birthed as the result of my own search for truth and the confusion I have experienced through the teachings of many, both historic and contemporary. I hope that, regardless of the conclusions I express, it will be helpful to those who are desirous of something more satisfying than the usual arguments, often based on superficial knowledge of the subject.

Throughout this book I have used the principle for studying prophecy as established by Dr David L. Cooper, that...

> *When the plain sense of scripture makes common sense we should seek no other sense, therefore we should take every word written in its primary, usual, ordinary and literal sense unless the evidence of the immediate context when studied in the light of the related passages and self-evident, fundamental truth would indicate otherwise.*

I have followed this principle despite the many varied interpretations of others, some of which I have drawn attention to. It must be understood that this is not a comprehensive review of the times and events of the Eschatology of the 'Last Days', for such would constitute a much larger and deeper investigation. The focus in this book is on the Book of Revelation alone, apart from a few minor supporting deviations. Note that some, but far from all, of the appropriate Old Testament prophecy references have been inserted, in brackets, at the end of comments relating to individual verses.

CHAPTER 1

The theme of the Revelation established – verses 1 to 8

¹The Revelation of Jesus Christ, which God gave Him to show His servants – things which must shortly take place. And He sent and signified it by His angel to His servant John, ²who bore witness to the word of God, and to the testimony of Jesus Christ, to all things that he saw. ³Blessed is he who reads and those who hear the words of this prophecy, and keep those things which are written in it; for the time is near. ⁴John, to the seven churches which are in Asia: Grace to you and peace from Him who is and who was and who is to come, and from the seven Spirits who are before His throne, ⁵and from Jesus Christ, the faithful witness, the firstborn from the dead, and the ruler over the kings of the earth. To Him who loved us and washed us from our sins in His own blood, ⁶and has made us kings and priests to His God and Father, to Him be glory and dominion forever and ever. Amen. ⁷Behold, He is coming with clouds, and every eye will see Him, even they who pierced Him. And all the tribes of the earth will mourn because of Him. Even so, Amen. ⁸'I am the Alpha and the Omega, the Beginning and the End,' says the Lord, 'who is and who was and who is to come, the Almighty.'

Verse 1: The words '*The Revelation of Jesus Christ*' in this verse do not mean that Yeshua is the object here, standing as one revealed, but that He is the One who is the revealer, or the One who is the author of what is to follow and written by John. It is not a revelation of Yeshua given by another, but a revelation which Yeshua Himself gives. It is a revelation, available to us through John, made either by Yeshua, or by an angel operating as mediator on His behalf. The word *'must'* in this verse indicates that what is to be revealed is something determined by divine will and of necessity it will happen. The most likely interpretation of the words *'must shortly take place'* is that they speak of the speed with which the things prophesied will happen when the time is right for them to be fulfilled. It does not necessarily mean that they are imminent, no dates are given, and no timescale is provided. There are some theologians who see the *'angel'* as being Yeshua in person but, in the light of subsequent references, this idea will not do and it must surely be that this angel is just an angel, who does not appear again until chapter 17, verse 1. (Daniel 2:28-29)

Verse 2: This verse tells us that John bore witness to the *'word of God'*, where it truly is the word of God that constitutes his testimony in this book, and which is the full gospel of Yeshua the Messiah. It is the testimony of Yeshua that is the 'Spirit of Prophecy' (see chapter 19, verse 10), and which forms the basis for all the things which John saw and has recorded in this book.

Verse 3: The Greek word *'kairos'* in this verse (meaning a specified period of time) was used by John in the phrase *'for the time is near'*. The significance of the word *'near'* is explained in the same sense as *'shortly'*, found in verse 1. This is the first of several blessings found in this book where, in this instance, it means blessings for those who read or hear and obey, and John obviously believed that what he wrote would be read to or by the Messianic communities.

Verse 4: With the words *'Him who is and who was and who is to come'*, addressed to the seven churches in Asia, John was defining the nature of God as being immutable and unchangeable, and it is this that distinguishes the Father from the Son in this instance. But it raises a question too, for who is it *'who is to come'*? We have just mentioned the nature of God, but this element must surely be speaking of Yeshua, the Messiah and coming King. However, bearing in mind that the Father and the Son are one, the One coming is Yeshua Himself. That God will come Himself, as some say, is probably not the correct understanding. The question of who or what constitutes the seven spirits will be discussed when we get to chapter 4. (Isaiah 11:2)

Verse 5a: In the first part of verse 5 we have Yeshua described as the *'faithful witness'*, faithful in that He made known to everyone all that which He heard from God the Father, and always spoke the truth no matter what the circumstances, even in the events leading to His death. He was *'the firstborn from the dead'* in that, following His death, He rose to life eternal and has pre-eminence over all things. This statement implies that, by being *'first'*, there will be others who will also rise to life eternal. Lazarus was raised from the dead, as a sign to Yeshua's critics, only to die again naturally later, but that was not the final end for him. Then, in addition, Yeshua is *'the ruler over the kings of the earth'*, something that He is right now and confirming that there is no rule or authority that exists without His permission, but will be more so when He personally returns and destroys the Antichrist, proving Himself through the times of judgement that are to come. (Genesis 49:11; Psalm 89:27)

Verses 5b & 6: The latter part of verse 5 has, in many Bibles, been translated in the wrong tense, i.e., that He *'loved'* us. The oldest manuscripts read that *'He did love us'*, in the present tense, the accent being more on *'love'* than on *'did'*. This is the true meaning and describes the permanent aspects of His nature and character. He loves all mankind, especially those who truly believe, and will always love us. The next phrase *'and has made us kings'*, found in verse 6, can hardly be taken to mean that believers will become kings in their own right, since there is only one King. It should more correctly be interpreted to mean that we become part of the kingdom of God and sharers in it, reigning with Him in the Millennium. But it is different when we read *'and priests to His God and Father'* because all believers will have direct access to God, the God of Yeshua, and they can offer their prayers and sacrifices in their holy service to Him. In this instance 'sacrifices' means the offering of our gifts and talents, not the blood of animals. Reference to the priesthood in Isaiah 61:6 and 1 Peter 2:9 apply to Israel only, it is only in these verses in Revelation that the church is included. Finally, in this verse, *'to Him be glory and dominion forever and ever. Amen,'* is speaking of none other than Yeshua Himself.

Verse 7: It is this verse that contains the theme for this Book of Revelation or, as it is called in Greek, *Apocalupsis*, from which we get Apocalypse (an understanding frequently misused when any disaster may be called 'apocalyptic'). When it says *'He is coming'* it is speaking of Yeshua who, at His Second Coming, will come *'with clouds'* where the clouds are from heaven and are symbolic of God's wrath. There are those who believe that the clouds symbolise the *'saints'*, both Jewish and Gentile, who will appear with Him after that period known as the Great Tribulation is over, but this is not logical. The clouds are real and identify the glory of God, revealing His wrath. The words *'... and every eye will see Him'* confirm that His Second Coming will be recognised universally, its effect being visible all around the world. The next phrase, *'... even they who pierced Him'*, may be speaking of all those, Jews and Gentiles alike of all the ages, who have rejected Him, but it is more likely that these words are speaking of the Jewish leaders who were responsible for His death, and all their descendants through the ages until the present time. *'And all the tribes of the earth will mourn because of Him. Even so, Amen.'* Here, in this verse, we have the fulfilment of the words found in Zechariah 12:10:

> And I will pour on the house of David and on the inhabitants of Jerusalem the Spirit of grace and supplication; then they will look on Me whom they pierced. Yes, they will mourn for Him as one mourns for his only son, and grieve for Him as one grieves for a firstborn.

...and there is also the allusion to Matthew 24:29–30, where the mourning is categorically stated as being after the Tribulation period:

> [29]Immediately after the tribulation of those days shall the sun be darkened, and the moon shall not give her light, and the stars shall fall from heaven, and the powers of the heavens shall be shaken: [30]And then shall appear the sign of the Son of man in heaven: and then shall all the tribes of the earth mourn, and they shall see the Son of man coming in the clouds of heaven with power and great glory.

Those who mourn most of all will be the Jewish people when, at last, the blindfold that has hidden the Messiah from their sight is removed, they recognise the disastrous mistake that was made, and they cry out for their Redeemer to come and deliver them. The Tribulation period of God's wrath is intended for this very purpose and the words *'Even so, Amen',* confirm that God's intent will be totally fulfilled. That Gentiles will also experience the tribulation of that time is without question, and many who are hostile or indifferent to the Gospel of Yeshua will perish, as we shall later see.

Verse 8: Here we have God Himself speaking, although some argue that it is Yeshua, and that may be so for He is all that this verse says, but that it is God is the most universally accepted interpretation. He is the One who existed at the beginning and will exist throughout eternity, the One who will come to Israel and to the Gentiles, in the form of the God/Man, to redeem His people. (Isaiah 41:4)

The vision of the Son of Man – verses 9 to 18

⁹I, John, both your brother and companion in the tribulation and kingdom and patience of Jesus Christ, was on the island that is called Patmos for the word of God and for the testimony of Jesus Christ. ¹⁰I was in the Spirit on the Lord's Day, and I heard behind me a loud voice, as of a trumpet, ¹¹saying, 'I am the Alpha and the Omega, the First and the Last,' and, 'What you see, write in a book and send it to the seven churches which are in Asia: to Ephesus, to Smyrna, to Pergamos, to Thyatira, to Sardis, to Philadelphia, and to Laodicea.' ¹²Then I turned to see the voice that spoke with me. And having turned I saw seven golden lampstands, ¹³and in the midst of the seven lampstands One like the Son of Man, clothed with a garment down to the feet and girded about the chest with a golden band. ¹⁴His head and hair were white like wool, as white as snow, and His eyes like a flame of fire; ¹⁵His feet were like fine brass, as if refined in a furnace, and His voice as the sound of many waters; ¹⁶He had in His right hand seven stars, out of His mouth went a sharp two-edged sword, and His countenance was like the sun shining in its strength. ¹⁷And when I saw Him, I fell at His feet as dead. But He laid His right hand on me, saying to me, 'Do not be afraid; I am the First and the Last. ¹⁸I am He who lives, and was dead, and behold, I am alive forevermore. Amen. And I have the keys of Hades and of Death.'

Verse 9: John, in this verse, introduces himself, and shares that because of what had happened to him in the period of tribulation following the death of Yeshua, how he had been imprisoned on the island of Patmos, where his present situation was all because of his testimony of Yeshua the Messiah.

Verse 10: John now goes on to say when his vision had begun, as he wrote, '*I was in the Spirit on the Lord's Day*', but exactly which day of the week that was is open to debate. In the original Greek the words '*the Lord's Day*' means, quite literally, '*a day belonging to the Lord*', which leaves open to question which day of the week he was referring to. The contention is that it could be any day, a day that John had set aside for personal worship. That understanding applies equally today. Whichever day of the week it was, it was on that day that John wrote, '*I heard behind me a loud voice, as of a trumpet*'.

Verse 11: We now learn what the voice behind him said: '*I am the Alpha and the Omega, the First and the Last,*' although we should note that some manuscripts omit this clause, but it is correctly included by the majority. John is, however, commissioned to write in a book, more probably a scroll, all that is to be shown him. He is then to send his book to the seven churches that are named. Why these seven in particular is unclear, for there were many other churches within the Roman Empire at that time. It could be because the number seven signifies totality and completeness, but it is also probable that these seven were representative of all the churches which, in themselves, embody the chief spiritual characteristics of the church through the ages, whether as faithful or unfaithful.

That these churches were not selected at random is fairly obvious for, together, they have a seven-sided wholeness. On one side there was Ephesus, intolerant of evil and false apostles, yet having lost its first love; on another there was Smyrna, a church experiencing persecutions unto death; on another side there was Pergamos, in conflict with those promoting fornication and idolatry. On the other hand, however, there was Thyatira, abounding in good works, love, service, and faith, yet permitting the false prophetess – whoever she was – to seduce many. Sardis, the next named, had gained a reputation for spiritual life but still it was dead. But then there was Philadelphia, with only a little strength, yet keeping Yeshua's word and having an open door of usefulness set before it by the Lord Himself. Finally there was Laodicea, in its own estimation rich and needing nothing, having many talents, but yet lukewarm in the cause of the Messiah, and spiritually destitute.

Verses 12 & 13: In verse 12 John turned, he says, to ascertain where the voice came from and to see who it was who was speaking to him. In turning, he saw seven lampstands all standing separately and representing the entire church but also signifying their mutual independence. The lampstands themselves are not the light; they are only the bearers of the light, holding it high to spread abroad its brightness. The light here is that of the Lord, not the individual churches, and it is from Him that they receive it. The church is therefore intended to be the light-bearer of His glory. Then, in the midst of the lampstands, was One who looked like the Son of Man, in the form John had seen Him at Gethsemane and on Calvary's hill, but now His glory was fully revealed, the direct consequence of His humiliation and cruel death as the Son of Man. (Daniel 10:5-6).

Verse 14: John described as best he could what he saw – the head and hair of this figure white like wool. The aspect of the wool is not clear but the colour is, for white signifies purity and glory, not old age. And then we learn that His eyes were like flame, burning, searching and penetrating just as fire does, which implies an all-consuming anger against sin. This will be manifested by Yeshua, for this is who it is, when He comes to take vengeance on all the ungodly at His Second Coming as we may read in 2 Thessalonians 2:7–8...*⁷For the mystery of iniquity doth already work: only he who now letteth will let, until he be taken out of the way. ⁸And then shall that Wicked be revealed, whom the Lord shall consume with the spirit of his mouth, and shall destroy with the brightness of his coming:*'(Daniel 7:9 KJV)

Verse 15: Continuing with his description John saw that *'His feet were like fine brass, as if refined in a furnace'.* Fine brass, from the Greek understanding, means brass that is flashing and white, as though white-hot from a furnace. That this was Yeshua is obvious and He, as our High Priest, was ministering with bare feet just as did the priests ministering in the temple. And His voice was like the sound of a roaring torrent, or waterfall, majestic and terrible in the ears of the wicked. (Ezekiel 43:2)

Verse 16: '*He had in His right hand seven stars...*' says John, which suggests not seven separate stars but seven stars joined together in some way, possibly as a crown. And '*... out of His mouth went a sharp two-edged sword...*', not held in the hand as one might expect. This sword can be interpreted as being the Sword of the Spirit, expressing His word and executing His judgements rather than its use in converting souls. Note that it is a two-edged sword, as the writer in Hebrews 4:12 puts it, '*piercing even to the dividing asunder of soul and spirit, and of the joints and marrow, and is a discerner of the thoughts and intents of the heart.*' Finally he says '*... and His countenance was like the sun shining in its strength*', in other words, the sun in its fullest and most brilliant splendour, its rays not obscured by clouds or in any way intercepted. (Isaiah 49:2)

Verse 17: In the presence of such glory and holiness John '*fell at His feet as dead*', the natural response of fallen man when faced with the manifestation of His glorious presence, and it overwhelmed him. '*But He laid His right hand on me,*' said John, the hand of comfort, imparting strength, just as Yeshua had done to His disciples on the Mount of Transfiguration, of whom John was one. He heard the words '*Do not be afraid; I am the First and the Last...*' spoken to him, revealing Yeshua's existence from eternity to eternity. (Daniel 10:19)

Verse 18: The voice continued, from verse 17, saying '*I am He who lives, and was dead, and behold, I am alive forevermore*' but, from the Greek, the correct translation of the words spoken here are '*... and the living one who was dead and behold, I am alive unto the ages of ages*'. The understanding of this is that Yeshua is the source of all life to every one of His people because He has life eternal in Himself. One theologian of the past puts it like this: 'To Him belongs absolute being, as contrasted with the relative being of the creature; others may share, He only hath immortality: being in essence, not by mere participation, immortal'[1]. And Yeshua holds '*the keys of Hades and of Death*'. '*Hades*' is a Greek word, found only in the New Testament, in

---

1   Richard Chenevix Trench DD. In his book, Epistles to the Seven Churches in Asia (New York: Charles Scribner, 1863).

ten passages in Matthew, Luke, Acts and Revelation, and identifies the spirit world of the dead.

There are seven conclusions that can be made from the passages where this word is found:

- *Hades* is the Greek equivalent of the Hebrew word *Sheol*, thus all that is true of one applies equally to the other.

- It was the place of both the righteous and the unrighteous dead, i.e., the rich man of Luke 16 on the one hand, and Yeshua Himself on the other.

- *Hades*, or *Sheol*, has two main compartments, each distinct, one for the unbelievers, generally called 'hell', and the other for the believers, called 'Paradise', which is also known as 'Abraham's Bosom.' (Luke 16:19–31)

- It will be very unpleasant for the unbeliever. (Matthew 11:24)

- The direction to it is always downward. (Matthew 11:23)

- It is a place of awareness, all will know where they are, and why. (Luke 16:19–31)

- It is a temporary place, not eternal. (Revelation 20:11–15)

The word 'hell' is an English word that, at its roots, means 'to hide' or 'to cover over'. There is no Hebrew or Greek equivalent from which 'hell' has been derived, and so it is not the best word to describe the unseen world of evil, but it does have within its meaning the concepts of both *Sheol* and *Hades*. What we today might call 'hell' the Old Testament calls *Abbadon*, or 'the Pit', but it contains no element of *Tartarus* or the abyss, the abodes of fallen angels. Hell, therefore, is reserved for human beings, and these human beings are the unsaved, unbelieving people of this world. What are the conditions for those in hell?

- First, there is a total absence of righteousness.

- It is a place totally separated from God.

- It is a place where the inhabitants are awaiting judgement.

- It is a place of darkness.

- It is a place of torment.

'Death', however, is not a place, it is a condition brought about by sin, robbing man of his immortal birthright, and what Yeshua is saying in this verse is that He can release whoever He will from the unseen world of spirits (*Hades*), and from the penalty of death, through repentance. Keys are symbols of authority, and He can open and shut the gates of *Hades* as He wishes. (Hosea 13:14)

The three primary elements of the Book of Revelation – verses 19 and 20

19Write the things which you have seen, and the things which are, and the things which will take place after this. 20The mystery of the seven stars which you saw in My right hand, and the seven golden lampstands: The seven stars are the angels of the seven churches, and the seven lampstands which you saw are the seven churches.

Verse 19: John was now commanded to write three things, the things that he had seen (past tense) the things as they were at that time (present tense) and the things yet to be (future tense). It is in Revelation 1:9–20 that the things he had seen are recorded. Then, in Revelation 2 and 3, we have the things that were current to him and, finally, it is in Revelation 4 to 22 that we have the things yet to be.

Verse 20: John was then given the explanation for the seven stars and the seven lampstands. The seven stars signify the angels of the seven churches. By angels he means God's messengers and ambassadors to the seven churches, called angels here both in respect of their office, being the representatives of Yeshua, and of the holiness they show in both doctrine and life. The seven candlesticks which John saw are the seven churches mentioned in verse 11, although there is the suggestion that seven being the number of perfection this is speaking of all churches everywhere, all represented by these seven candlesticks.

CHAPTER 2

The letters to the seven churches

We have given thought to the things that John had seen, and we now move on to consider chapters 2 and 3, into the *'things that are'*. We shall find that these chapters describe the characteristics of the churches named, each having five characteristics in common. These are:

1. They each contain the last recorded and audible words of Yeshua.

2. The seven letters are addressed to the visible churches, made up of believers and unbelievers.

3. We shall also see that Yeshua is critical of five of the churches, but not of two of them.

4. But we shall find that six of the churches do have something good said about them, no matter how bad they are, but for one of them nothing good is said at all.

5. There are four things that all seven churches have in common, and they are these:

   i. Each one describes an aspect of Yeshua the Messiah as previously found in chapter 1.

ii.   In each letter Yeshua says, 'I know your works...' and in this context the word 'know' has the meaning 'knowing intimately'.

iii.   Yeshua, in each one, addresses the overcomer, followed by a promise.

iv.   He then says, 'He who has an ear...' where what follow are words to encourage the hearers to listen to and note the words that have been spoken.

The letter to the church at Ephesus – verses 1 to 7

¹To the angel of the church of Ephesus write, "These things says He who holds the seven stars in His right hand, who walks in the midst of the seven golden lampstands: ²I know your works, your labour, your patience, and that you cannot bear those who are evil. And you have tested those who say they are apostles and are not, and have found them liars; ³and you have persevered and have patience, and have laboured for My name's sake and have not become weary. ⁴Nevertheless I have this against you, that you have left your first love. ⁵Remember therefore from where you have fallen; repent and do the first works, or else I will come to you quickly and remove your lamp-stand from its place – unless you repent. ⁶But this you have, that you hate the deeds of the Nicolaitans, which I also hate. ⁷He who has an ear, let him hear what the Spirit says to the churches. To him who overcomes I will give to eat from the tree of life, which is in the midst of the Paradise of God."'

Verse 1: The name Ephesus means 'desired' or 'desired one' which has, no doubt, something to do with the fact that this was the city of the famous temple to Diana (also called Artemis), represented as a many-breasted mother goddess. That it is the first church to be addressed indicates that it was the most significant one, and certainly Ephesus was strategically, economically and religiously very important. Here again, in this verse, we have the description of Yeshua, a repeat of chapter 1, verses 16 and 13, and which relate to the nature of the Messiah. He is in control, it says, for He has the destiny of all the churches in His hand. We can see that this letter addresses a major issue that, even so early in church history, was becoming a problem – apostasy. However, Yeshua, in His commendation, speaks of the good things about this church.

Verses 2 & 3: We note that this church hated evil, tested and rejected the false prophets and despised the works of the Nicolaitans. We learn from these verses that this church resisted the false teachers, those apostates whose coming was foretold by Paul, in Acts 20:28–29. Timothy was pastoring the church in Ephesus at that time, combating the false prophets, but by the time we reach this chapter, and from John's letter here, it appears they had been dealt with and had been put out of the church.

Verse 4: We learn of the Lord's condemnation in this verse, *'You have left [or lost] your first love.'* When John was writing down this vision it was addressed to the second and third generations of believers and the condemnation was that they did not have the zeal or enthusiasm of the first generation. Such words presuppose a real danger of falling away and embracing once again the death-creating rules of Judaism. (Jeremiah 2:2)

Verse 5: Now, in this verse, we have the call that they should return to the zeal of their fathers. *'Remember therefore from where you have fallen'.* They should remember and consider it because of the risk factor, for Yeshua says, *'I will come to you quickly and remove your lamp-stand'.* The lampstand, or candlestick, is the sign or symbol of their witness to unbelievers, their testimony of what God had done in their lives. Yeshua warned that the lampstand and its light would disappear and they would then cease to be a witness at all for Yeshua.

Verse 6: But they do hate the activities of the Nicolaitans. That is obviously a good thing, although no one is quite sure why. The general belief is that this was a group that took their name from Nicolaus, an early follower, but who endeavoured to establish a compromise between the early believers and the paganism of the time to enable the believers to partake in the social activities of the pagans without embarrassment. They are believed to have advocated considerable relaxation of sexual and moral standards and ultimately to have hardened into a Gnostic, control-seeking sect. What this does seem to reveal is that within the early church there was an attempt to establish a clear distinction between those in authority and those who were not, between clergy and laity, which is something the Bible does not countenance. Only spiritual authority under God-anointed leadership is permitted.

Verse 7: The earlier condemnation is followed by a promise – or, to be more precise, two promises. First, as overcomers, they were guaranteed a place in the Eternal Order to come, they would *'eat from the tree of life'*... and they would enter into a special relationship with God, as they find themselves *'in the midst of the Paradise of God'*. What these two commissions mean we shall look at in greater detail on a later occasion. (Proverbs 13:12)

The letter to the church at Smyrna – verses 8 to 11

[8]And to the angel of the church in Smyrna write, "These things says the First and the Last, who was dead, and came to life: [9] I know your works, tribulation, and poverty (but you are rich); and I know the blasphemy of those who say they are Jews and are not, but are a synagogue of Satan. [10]Do not fear any of those things which you are about to suffer. Indeed, the devil is about to throw some of you into prison, that you may be tested, and you will have tribulation ten days. Be faithful until death, and I will give you the crown of life. [11]He who has an ear, let him hear what the Spirit says to the churches. He who overcomes shall not be hurt by the second death."'

Verse 8: Here the meaning of the name is 'myrrh', which is an extract from a small tree that grows in Arabia. The connotations of myrrh are death and embalming, which may be considered as fitting for a church that was soon to experience Roman persecution, something that actually took place during the period of 100 to 313AD. In this verse we again have the description of Yeshua, *'the First and the Last'*, which is found in verse 17 of chapter 1, and *'was dead, and came to life'* from verse 18. The emphasis here is on the death and resurrection of Yeshua – who died a violent death but overcame it by rising again and who now has authority over death and hell.

Verse 9: This church was soon to go through violence, torture and death, but would overcome in the same way that Yeshua overcame – through physical resurrection at some future time. There is commendation for this church in two specific areas. The first is patience in the face of suffering and tribulation; the second is standing against the persecution of those who claimed to be Jews but were not.

This latter statement probably needs some clarification. Throughout scripture the 'people of God' are the Jewish nation, there is no doubt about that. But when Yeshua was speaking here of those claiming to be Jews He was actually referring to those who were claiming they were 'the people of god'. But at this time in history those who said they were the people of god were, in fact, the Romans. Any who professed allegiance to Rome were required, under penalty of death, to accept the deity of the emperor and to worship him. So it was by virtue of their belief in their emperor as being a god that they claimed to be the 'people of god' and yet tried to identify with the believers. It was because the church at Smyrna rejected such claims that they were commended for it. This was one of the churches that Yeshua had nothing against – the consequence of this is that there was no condemnation.

Verse 10: In this verse the people are encouraged not to fear the coming of suffering, but they were then warned of ten days of severe persecution that was going to come upon the church. In Roman times these were ten specific days of really terrible persecution in the lives of individual believers who were challenged to worship the emperor as god and many who did not would then be executed. The exhortation continues, '*Be faithful unto death*', and those who were and will be faithful could and can expect to receive the crown of life.

Verse 11: This verse records the promise given to this church. They were told that although they might die violently, their death, through faith in Yeshua, would preserve them from the '*second death*'. What that term means we shall review in some detail later on. This is the sure promise for those who will be overcomers, but for those who were responsible for the persecution, and for the torture and killing, there would be no such promise when they stood before the judgement seat. They would be consigned to the '*second death*', which meant eternity in the 'Lake of Fire'. This is the place prepared for Satan and his evil angels, not a lake as such but a place of eternal torment, to which he has not yet been consigned. This will not happen until the final judgement, described in chapter 20, mentioned here to show what will be his final state and condition.

The letter to the church at Pergamos – verses 12 to 17

¹²'And to the angel of the church in Pergamos write, "These things says He who has the sharp two-edged sword: ¹³I know your works, and where you dwell, where Satan's throne is. And you hold fast to My name, and did not deny My faith even in the days in which Antipas was My faithful martyr, who was killed among you, where Satan dwells. ¹⁴But I have a few things against you, because you have there those who hold the doctrine of Balaam, who taught Balak to put a stumbling block before the children of Israel, to eat things sacrificed to idols, and to commit sexual immorality. ¹⁵Thus you also have those who hold the doctrine of the Nicolaitans, which thing I hate. ¹⁶Repent, or else I will come to you quickly and will fight against them with the sword of My mouth. ¹⁷He who has an ear, let him hear what the Spirit says to the churches. To him who overcomes I will give some of the hidden manna to eat. And I will give him a white stone, and on the stone a new name written which no one knows except him who receives it."'

Verse 12: The description of Yeshua, taken from chapter 1, verse 16, speaks of Him exercising judgement by the sword. The angel is saying here that Yeshua alone possesses the ultimate authority, as represented by the *'sharp two-edged sword'*. It was here in this city that the Roman proconsul exercised his authority by the use of the sword. The name Pergamos, or Pergamum, has the meaning 'thoroughly married', and this Greco/Roman city is also identified as the location of 'The Seat of Satan'. The reference to Satan's throne may apply to an actual seat, but it is more likely that it was an altar to Zeus used for cultic worship. In the late nineteenth century, and in conjunction with the Turkish authorities, this monument was dismantled and moved to Germany, where it was located in the Pergamon Museum in Berlin. 'The Pergamon Museum is situated on the Museum Island in Berlin. The site was designed by Alfred

Messel and Ludwig Hoffmann and was constructed in twenty years, from 1910 to 1930.'[2] Was that significant in the light of what later happened? (Isaiah 49:2)

Verse 13: There are two areas for which the church at Pergamos was commended. Here Yeshua says, *'You held fast to my name and you did not deny My faith'*. All this was despite being in the place where Satan's throne was situated. This city was the centre of pagan worship and one cult was of particular significance – the cult of Asclepius Soter, a name that means 'serpent', 'saviour' and 'healer'. He was represented by a figure half-man, half-serpent and we know that, in scripture, a serpent equates to Satan, so it may well have been for this reason that Pergamos gained fame as the centre of satanic worship.

Verse 14: There are two areas where the church in Pergamos had failed and which justified the Lord's condemnation. In this verse that condemnation is addressed to the fact that they had been holding fast to the teachings of Balaam. We can read all about this character in Numbers 22–24, where he can be described as an astrologer, or seer, in Babylonia. What Yeshua is pointing out in this situation is that the spirit introduced by Balaam was active right there throughout the unity between church and state because of the fornication and idolatry that was accepted as normal.

The result of all this was that, since Christianity had become the state religion of the Roman Empire, being a believing Christian was not one of the best things to be, for it was now obligatory to be a member of the church. The way in to the church was through baptism, but not believer's baptism, since just by being baptised you were accepted regardless of what you believed. Thus it was that whole tribes and families of pagans were being accepted into the church simply on the basis of being baptised, without being asked the question, 'Do you believe?' (Numbers 25:1-3)

Verse 15: Here we have the second area of condemnation, the acceptance of the teaching and methods of the Nicolaitans. We have already learned something about this group from the church at Ephesus. During this period a priestly structure was being

---

2   Source: Wikipedia.

installed within the church and Nicolaitan principles were being introduced. One of these principles was in the area of control and now, with the setting up of a priestly order, came the exercising of control by the priests over the laity. It became a situation where the rights of the individual were bypassed by the authoritarianism of the priests, as we know, and has been evident in the more recent history of the church through what is called 'heavy shepherding'. It was this that the Lord condemned, and does today just as He did then.

Verse 16: This verse reveals the Lord's exhortation – repent, or else! Repentance was essential here, and quickly too, for the threat of destruction existed, certainly for those who compromised over the things Yeshua hated. Reference again to *'the sword of My mouth'* is speaking of sharp retribution.

Verse 17: In this verse we have three promises – hidden *manna*, a white stone and a new name. For an individual, a family or a group to have withdrawn from the church in protest would have resulted in isolation and loss of livelihood, but the promise of the *manna* is saying that if any did quit for the right reasons, God would make provision for them as He did for the Israelites in the wilderness. The white stone had two meanings in those days:

1. If the white stone was presented by the judge at a trial it meant acquittal.

2. It was the sign of acceptance to anyone who had applied for membership of a private guild.

The main emphasis of these promises is future and these aspects will apply for all believers today and during the coming time of tribulation. We are and we shall be acquitted from judgement, and we shall be accepted by God even if not by the church. Finally God will give a new name to all who overcome in the spiritual realm, take Jacob for instance, as he returned from Mesopotamia and struggled with God by the brook Jabbok, and was given a new name, Israel, from which came the name of a nation. (Genesis 32:28)

The letter to the church at Thyatira – verses 18 to 29

¹⁸‘And to the angel of the church in Thyatira write, "These things says the Son of God, who has eyes like a flame of fire, and His feet like fine brass: ¹⁹I know your works, love, service, faith, and your patience; and as for your works, the last are more than the first. ²⁰Nevertheless I have a few things against you, because you allow that woman Jezebel, who calls herself a prophetess, to teach and seduce My servants to commit sexual immorality and eat things sacrificed to idols. ²¹And I gave her time to repent of her sexual immorality, and she did not repent. ²²Indeed I will cast her into a sickbed, and those who commit adultery with her into great tribulation, unless they repent of their deeds. ²³I will kill her children with death, and all the churches shall know that I am He who searches the minds and hearts. And I will give to each one of you according to your works. ²⁴Now to you I say, and to the rest in Thyatira, as many as do not have this doctrine, who have not known the depths of Satan, as they say, I will put on you no other burden. ²⁵But hold fast what you have till I come. ²⁶And he who overcomes, and keeps My works until the end, to him I will give power over the nations – ²⁷'He shall rule them with a rod of iron; They shall be dashed to pieces like the potter's vessels' – as I also have received from My Father; ²⁸and I will give him the morning star. ²⁹He who has an ear, let him hear what the Spirit says to the churches."’

Verse 18: This letter is addressed to the church at Thyatira, where the name means 'perpetual sacrifice'. This is a particularly fitting epithet for the period of history that we can identify with this church, known as 'the Dark Ages' (600–1570AD). It can be seen particularly in Roman Catholic doctrine in regard to the Mass, where prayer over the bread and wine of the communion supposedly causes the elements to actually become the body and blood of Yeshua. This means that every time Mass is celebrated Catholics are effectively re-enacting Calvary all over again. But Yeshua's death was a once and for all sacrifice, so this is a fundamental area of error.

It has changed a little now, but it was often used as a pretext for anti-Semitism and campaigns against Jewish communities. Priests would make false accusations against the Jews, saying they had broken into the church, stolen the elements and had nailed them to a tree – just as they believed it was the Jews who had nailed Yeshua to the cross, hence re-crucifying the Lord. It was on this flimsy accusation that so many pogroms began when thousands of innocent men, women and children were slaughtered in the name of Yeshua. The name of Thyatira, therefore, shows the 'continuing sacrifice' of Yeshua.

Verse 19: The commendation is fairly brief, saying that their works of love, service, faith and patience had increased from what they were, but in...

Verse 20: ... there is the condemnation. They tolerated the activities of *'that woman Jezebel'*. Does this refer to a particular woman of that time, to a group, or to some spiritual activity? It appears that 'she' is a prophetess and a seducer, but what else do we know? The first Jezebel is described in 1 Kings as the daughter of Ethbaal, priest-king of Tyre and Sidon. As the wife of Ahab, the king of Israel, she was a strong, domineering and ambitious woman seeking total authority for the monarchy, and for herself, which was at variance with the traditional Hebrew covenantal relationship between God, the king and the people. She was deeply into idolatry and, although not the first to introduce idol worship into Israel, she did bring a new god, Baal, and 450 of his 'prophets' as well as 400 'prophets' of the goddess Asherah. (1 Kings 16:31-32)

Verse 21: The 'woman' was given time to repent, but she did not. The judgement that would fall upon this false teaching is clearly defined in verses 22 and 23, where we find it in two parts.

Verse 22: First we have the judgement of the Jezebel spirit that is evident in Roman Catholicism, and in much of the visible, apostate, church too, which, without true repentance, will go through what is called 'the Great Tribulation'.

Verse 23: Then we see that the followers of this creed, and adherents to it, will suffer violence and death during the Tribulation period, and the visible, apostate church will not escape from this judgement. (Psalm 28:4)

Verses 24 & 25: Yeshua's exhortation, addressed to those who have not become involved in the things of Satan, can be found in these verses. At this point in history the church in Rome had become Satan's counterfeit of the true religion, but Yeshua said He would not add to the church's problems, that they were not to do anything new but just to stand fast. With the circumstances as they were, that in itself would be something special, a huge task. With the words *'But hold fast what you have till I come',* Yeshua is speaking of His Second Coming, an exhortation applying equally to believers today.

Verses 26 to 29: Here we have the promises. The first of these tells the members of this church that they would receive a part in the Millennial Kingdom. It would be there that Yeshua would give them authority to rule over the nations. It was from this point on that the Church of Rome began to exercise more and more authority in the political realm, the result of merging state and church in many nations. But Yeshua is saying that this was not real authority, it was bogus and counterfeit. The real authority will be given to the overcomers in such a situation, authority that is truly divine in origin. The Morning Star is the Lord Yeshua Himself, who is saying to believers that the only way to overcome in this problem, generated by the church of Rome, is to receive the salvation Yeshua offers, the true faith, because in possessing salvation we also possess the nature of Yeshua and the fullness of the Godhead. (Isaiah 30:14)

CHAPTER 3

The letter to the church at Sardis –
verses 1 to 6

¹And to the angel of the church in Sardis write, "These things says He who has the seven Spirits of God and the seven stars: 'I know your works, that you have a name that you are alive, but you are dead. ²Be watchful, and strengthen the things which remain, that are ready to die, for I have not found your works perfect before God. ³Remember therefore how you have received and heard; hold fast and repent. Therefore if you will not watch, I will come upon you as a thief, and you will not know what hour I will come upon you. ⁴You have a few names even in Sardis who have not defiled their garments; and they shall walk with Me in white, for they are worthy. ⁵He who overcomes shall be clothed in white garments, and I will not blot out his name from the Book of Life; but I will confess his name before My Father and before His angels. ⁶He who has an ear, let him hear what the Spirit says to the churches.'"

Verse 1: The destination for the fifth letter is the church in Sardis. The name of this city means 'those escaping' which we may consider apt in that the period in church history represented here is the Reformation. The description of Yeshua is taken from chapter 1, verses 4, 16 and 20, and emphasises that it is both Yeshua and the Holy Spirit that are opposed to this church which was spiritually dead. In this verse we again find a condemnation, *'I know your works...but you are dead'*.

Verses 2 & 3: Yeshua exhorts the Sardis church in these verses. All the good works, however sincerely performed, would never achieve the desired perfection; they would always fall short. The call upon them was to resuscitate those things before it was too late and the death of that which was dying would actually occur. There was, at the beginning, personal faith as we see, from the words *'Remember therefore how you have received and heard'*... but this faith had been lost by successive generations because spiritual life had declined to zero. All this can be summed up as plenty of traditionalism, good doctrine and a sound creed, but nothing of the Spirit. Yeshua also said that if no attempt was made to put the situation right and the way to death was not reversed, He would come without warning to bring His judgement. Of course, spiritual life without sound doctrine means error and deception, amongst other things, but sound doctrine without spiritual life is cold and dead.

Verse 4: The members of this church, those who have endured by faith, are the recipients of a three part promise – as recorded in verse 5. (Ecclesiates 9:8)

Verse 5: Here are the promises. The first is that those who overcame would be clothed in white garments. We shall later see that white robes are the sign of justification and salvation. This promise identifies the problems of the Sardis church – that only the few, the overcomers, would be clothed in the white robes. The others, despite their good creed and sound doctrine, had no spiritual life and therefore no hope. But to those who truly believed, there was a future salvation. So, thankfully, there will be some today, from within dead churches, who will be saved. Their names will not be blotted out from the Book of Life, which makes it clear that those whose names are not included among them will find themselves at a considerable disadvantage. Finally, Yeshua will confess, or more correctly He will commend, the overcomers before God and His angels (See Luke 12:8). What a wonderful reward for remaining true to the gospel and the fundamentals of faith. (Exodus 32:32-33)

Verse 6: All of us are encouraged to take heed of what is said here.

The letter to the church at Philadelphia – verses 7 to 13

⁷'And to the angel of the church in Philadelphia write, "These things says He who is holy, He who is true, He who has the key of David, He who opens and no one shuts, and shuts and no one opens: ⁸I know your works. See, I have set before you an open door, and no one can shut it; for you have a little strength, have kept My word, and have not denied My name. ⁹Indeed I will make those of the synagogue of Satan, who say they are Jews and are not, but lie – indeed I will make them come and worship before your feet, and to know that I have loved you. ¹⁰Because you have kept My command to persevere, I also will keep you from the hour of trial which shall come upon the whole world, to test those who dwell on the earth. ¹¹Behold, I am coming quickly! Hold fast what you have, that no one may take your crown. ¹² He who overcomes, I will make him a pillar in the temple of My God, and he shall go out no more. And I will write on him the name of My God and the name of the city of My God, the New Jerusalem, which comes down out of heaven from My God. And I will write on him My new name. ¹³He who has an ear, let him hear what the Spirit says to the churches."'

Verse 7: The destination for this, the sixth letter, is the angel of the church at Philadelphia, a name meaning 'the city of brotherly love'. This was the first church established in Asia Minor, the result of earlier missionary activity. The description of Yeshua is confirmation of Revelation 1:18 – that it is Yeshua who has authority to open and close doors. Note that there is no condemnation. This was the second church not to be condemned for anything; the other was Smyrna. (Isaiah 22:22)

Verse 8: But there is commendation, for it then tells us they have made use of the open door, thus making possible the way to evangelisation.

Verse 9: Here we have the first promise – there will be converts from among those who claim to be Jews but are not. Alongside of their sound missionary activity there would always be the danger of cults growing and increasing their influence within the Christian movement, just as there is today, and all will claim to have found some connection with

Israel and to be Jews in some form or another, but such claims are false. (Isaiah 60:14)

Verse 10: The second promise, Yeshua says, is for the overcomers when the *'hour of trial'* would come upon them, which is another way of saying 'the Great Tribulation', for He will keep them *'from'* it. Not *'through'* it, as might be expected and some believe, but *'from'* it. There may well have been an *'hour of trial'*, or maybe several, for the people of the church at Philadelphia, in which case the promises may mean no more than being safeguarded during the difficult periods, and this must also be true for all the periods of church history prior to the Great Tribulation.

Modern history, and the situation today in many nations where Christians suffer greatly, might suggest this promise has been ineffective. But in the context of the words *'come upon the whole world'*, the meaning must surely relate to the Tribulation period, which leads us to the belief that the true church, those who overcome, will be kept from it by being raptured before it begins.

Verse 11: In this verse we find the exhortation – hang in there! Merely to keep going the way they have been, for when Yeshua comes, He will come quickly – and He is coming, that's guaranteed.

Verse 12: We now have the description of the third and fourth promises. The overcomer will become a beautiful and effective part of the Millennial temple, trusted and true, and then, finally, we read that he/she will be given a new name. That name is the name of God, the name given to Yeshua and also the name given to the New Jerusalem.

In the sense that in Jewish culture the name given says something of the nature of the person bearing it, we can derive from this scripture what the name of the overcomer will be. One of the names of God is *Jehovah Tsidkenu*, meaning 'God our Righteousness' and it is this name that is then applied to the Messiah (Jeremiah 23:6), and also to the New Jerusalem (Jeremiah 33:16). This promise, then, must surely mean that the true believers, at the moment they receive that name, will take on not just the name but the righteousness of God when they take up their place in the Millennial Kingdom. (Ezekiel 48:35)

Verse 13: Again the exhortation to hear and take note.

The letter to the church at Laodicea – verses 14 to 22

[14]'And to the angel of the church of the Laodiceans write, "These things says the Amen, the Faithful and True Witness, the Beginning of the creation of God: [15]I know your works, that you are neither cold nor hot. I could wish you were cold or hot [16]So then, because you are lukewarm, and neither cold nor hot, I will vomit you out of My mouth. [17]Because you say, "I am rich, have become wealthy, and have need of nothing" – and do not know that you are wretched, miserable, poor, blind, and naked – [18]I counsel you to buy from Me gold refined in the fire, that you may be rich; and white garments, that you may be clothed, that the shame of your nakedness may not be revealed; and anoint your eyes with eye salve, that you may see. [19]As many as I love, I rebuke and chasten. Therefore be zealous and repent. [20]Behold, I stand at the door and knock. If anyone hears My voice and opens the door, I will come in to him and dine with him, and he with Me. [21]To him who overcomes I will grant to sit with Me on My throne, as I also overcame and sat down with My Father on His throne. [22]He who has an ear, let him hear what the Spirit says to the churches."'

Verse 14: The seventh and final letter is addressed to the church in Laodicea, a name that means 'people ruling'. The description of Yeshua can be compared with that found in chapter 1, verses 5 and 8. He is the one who is faithful and true, not something that could be said about this particular church.

Verse 15: For this church there was no commendation, nothing at all for which any words of encouragement could possibly apply. There was only the implication that repentance would be beneficial, and suggesting that through it there might be those who would, or could, become overcomers.

Verse 16: But of condemnation there was much. They were condemned for their lukewarmness. No doubt Yeshua was referring indirectly to the hot springs of Hieropolis and the cold waters of Collossae, to the healing and refreshing qualities of these. To vomit them, that is the Laodiceans, out of His mouth seems to suggest that He would cast them off as unclean.

Verse 17: They were worldly and materialistic. This was a self-sufficient and self-confident apostate church, rather than half-hearted, and was convinced it needed nothing but, in fact, it had nothing and was spiritually destitute.

Summarising, then, in the content of the condemnation of this church, we may see that this letter has five aspects:

1. It is prophetic in terms of the apostasy to come.

2. It reveals the character of apostasy.

3. It shows the mark of apostasy.

4. It describes the work of apostasy.

5. It details the history of apostasy.

What is apostasy? It simply means rebellion against God and departure from the truth of God's word. This church professed to have the truth, that they knew it, but they didn't possess it. They said that they had it all but didn't live it, and they departed from it. Are there parallels today? Sadly, yes.

Verse 18: In this verse we read of the Lord's exhortation. It is to anyone who will listen. They were advised to buy gold, the gold of obedience, *'gold refined in the fire'*, and to obtain white garments, the sign of righteousness and the symbol of salvation, so that their spiritual poverty might not be revealed, and to seek the *'eye salve'* of anointed vision. (Isaiah 55:1)

Verse 19: The thrust of what Yeshua was saying to the church of Laodicea is this – the apostate church will go the same way of the Jezebel church, but if anyone wants to pull out, to be separated from the corruption, the way to restoration was through repentance – and that's the clear message to the church today. (Proverbs 3:12)

Verse 20: Here is the promise to this church. The Lord is standing at the door of opportunity and for those who hear, by opening the door, they can have true fellowship with God.

Verse 21: The promise to the Laodiceans continues in this verse. For the overcomer there will be a place next to Yeshua, but not to be able to relax in comfort, for it will be a place of authority, a place of ruling and reigning.

Verse 22: Again the invitation is to hear what the Lord is saying.

CHAPTER 4

The things yet to be – verses 1 to 11

¹After these things I looked, and behold, a door standing open in heaven. And the first voice which I heard was like a trumpet speaking with me, saying, "Come up here, and I will show you things which must take place after this." ²Immediately I was in the Spirit; and behold, a throne set in heaven, and One sat on the throne. ³And He who sat there was like a jasper and a sardius stone in appearance; and there was a rainbow around the throne, in appearance like an emerald. ⁴Around the throne were twenty-four thrones, and on the thrones I saw twenty-four elders sitting, clothed in white robes; and they had crowns of gold on their heads. ⁵And from the throne proceeded lightnings, thunderings, and voices. Seven lamps of fire were burning before the throne, which are the seven Spirits of God. ⁶Before the throne there was a sea of glass, like crystal. And in the midst of the throne, and around the throne, were four living creatures full of eyes in front and in back. ⁷The first living creature was like a lion, the second living creature like a calf, the third living creature had a face like a man, and the fourth living creature was like a flying eagle. ⁸The four living creatures, each having six wings, were full of eyes around and within. And they do not rest day or night, saying: "Holy, holy, holy, Lord God Almighty, Who was and is and is to come!" ⁹Whenever the living creatures give glory and honour and thanks to Him who sits on the throne, who lives forever and ever, ¹⁰the twenty-four elders fall down before Him who sits on the throne *and worship Him who lives forever and ever, and cast their crowns before the throne, saying: ¹¹"You are worthy, O Lord, to receive glory and honour and power; for You created all things, and by Your will they exist and were created."*

Verse 1: John now saw, as it were, a door that was open, and he heard the command *'Come up here'*. These words were spoken as a specific invitation that was meant to be obeyed right then and were not, as some propose, words in general to be given to the whole church in the future at the time of the Rapture. In his vision John saw right into the heaven of heavens, although he does not explain much about it other than that he saw an open door, but that is surely enough for us to see that there will be an open door for the believers, an invitation that opens the way for all believers to enter in on a future occasion. Interestingly it does not tell us that he actually went in, only that he looked in, but that is how God frequently communicates through the visions given – you see, but you don't go! (Ezekiel 1:1)

Verses 2 & 3: John, through spiritual eyes, looked and saw a throne with someone sitting on it. It is interesting that he says here that he *'was in the Spirit'*. Surely he was in the Spirit already, so this seems to suggest that he was now experiencing a change in his position. He goes on to describe, as best he can in earthly terms, the impression that lay right before his eyes, the majesty, the beauty and the glory. (Ezekiel 1:26)

Verse 4: And then, around the throne, he saw twenty-four *'elders'*, each of them seated on a throne. How did he know they were elders? Is it that they must have been important because of their being so immediately in attendance upon God, or is it because they might have appeared to be old? Or perhaps they were obviously beings with great spiritual authority? Who were they, anyway? Were they celestial beings? Some sort of angels? Or could they be church saints? They were not the apostles, there were only twelve of those, plus Paul, and John would have recognised them if they were. The problem of identification is one that has demanded much attention over the years, but probably the best solution is the simplest, that they are, in fact, church saints. The reasons for offering this argument are:

1. Celestial beings (including *cherubim*, *seraphim* and angels) are never called *'elders'*, this term being used exclusively for men.

2. They are seen to be wearing white garments which, as we have already learned, is the sign that the wearers have attained full salvation. This rules out the celestial beings theory because they have never needed to attain salvation for the reason that they had never lost theirs in the first place.

3. They were wearing *stephanos* crowns, the sign of the overcomer, and not the *diademas* of royalty, as worn by the celestial beings.

All believer saints of all time, whether they are Jews or Gentiles, enter into Paradise when they die and remain there until the return of Yeshua to collect His bride through the Rapture, (2 Corinthians 5:8). If we believe that the elders seen by John are church saints, as representatives of all believers, and who are now in the presence of God, this must surely confirm a pre-Tribulation Rapture.

Verse 5: John now saw, among all the flashes and crashes and voices, seven lamps of fire. These are identified as the seven spirits of God. Seven? But God is Himself spirit and has only one spirit, the Holy Spirit, the third person of the Trinity. This must mean that the seven lamps represent seven aspects of the one Spirit. We find these aspects given to us in Isaiah 11:2. They are:

1. The Spirit of the Lord.

2. The Spirit of Wisdom.

3. The Spirit of Understanding.

4. The Spirit of Counsel.

5. The Spirit of Might.

6. The Spirit of Knowledge.

7. The Spirit of the Fear of the Lord.

Verse 6: There are many symbols throughout this book that are hard to interpret and here, in this verse, we have an example of this. John, in this verse, tells us that '*Before the throne there was a sea of glass, like crystal*', a description quite beyond our understanding. It is unlikely, as some say, that the sea represents the glorified church, and it is best if we just take it as it is written. It's what John saw. There, too, was a throne and around the throne were four living creatures full of eyes. (Ezekiel 1:5)

Verse 7: These creatures are described here but not named. It is their faces that seem to impress John the most, first a lion, then a calf, a man and an eagle. According to the ancient rabbis, the lion was the standard of Judah, Issachar and Zebulon, the calf or ox was the standard of Ephraim, Manasseh and Benjamin, the man was the standard of Reuben, Simeon and Gad and, finally, the eagle was the standard of Dan, Asher and Naphtali, but whether any of this has meaning is not clear. Especially take note of the link with Ezekiel's vision, (Ezekiel 10:14). Christian tradition, however, identifies these creatures as emblems of the apostles, of John (the eagle), of Luke (the calf), of Mark (the lion), and of Matthew (the man). Whether any of these latter understandings are the right ones is debatable.

Verse 8: John has added a little to the descriptions here. These beings each have six wings, lots of eyes, and do not rest, where their primary role is to declare the holiness of God. To find out who or what they are we must turn to Isaiah 6:2. There we are told they are seraphs (in Hebrew, '*seraphim*'), and we know this because they have six wings. We find there are three orders of celestial beings as we study the Bible – *cherubim* (the highest order), *seraphim*, and then angels – all identifiable by the number of their 'wings'. *Cherubim* have four, *seraphim* have six and, to most people's surprise, angels have none. Note that Lucifer (Satan) was a cherub, while Michael, an archangel, is of an order lower than the *cherubim* and the *seraphim*, having a different function.

Verse 9: The word '*Whenever*', found in this verse, means that as often as those living beings ascribe glory to God, and they did this continually, we have the impression that the ways and acts of God in His providential government are continually of such a nature as to deserve such honour. (Daniel 4:34)

Verse 10: The representatives of the redeemed church in heaven also unite in the praise. The meaning here is that the true church universal unites in praise to God for all that characterises His government and authority.

Verse 11: In this verse we may understand that all the praise, homage, and acknowledgment of the *seraphim* and of the elders is appropriate for God, the Creator of all things, and are His due. (Genesis 1:1)

CHAPTER 5

The Lamb and the seven sealed scroll – verses 1 to 14

[1]And I saw in the right hand of Him who sat on the throne a scroll written inside and on the back, sealed with seven seals. [2]Then I saw a strong angel proclaiming with a loud voice, "Who is worthy to open the scroll and to loose its seals?" [3]And no one in heaven or on the earth or under the earth was able to open the scroll, or to look at it. [4]So I wept much, because no one was found worthy to open and read the scroll, or to look at it. [5]But one of the elders said to me, "Do not weep. Behold, the Lion of the tribe of Judah, the Root of David, has prevailed to open the scroll and to loose its seven seals." [6]And I looked, and behold, in the midst of the throne and of the four living creatures, and in the midst of the elders, stood a Lamb as though it had been slain, having seven horns and seven eyes, which are the seven Spirits of God sent out into all the earth. [7]Then He came and took the scroll out of the right hand of Him who sat on the throne. [8]Now when He had taken the scroll, the four living creatures and the twenty-four elders fell down before the Lamb, each having a harp, and golden bowls full of incense, which are the prayers of the saints. [9]And they sang a new song, saying: "You are worthy to take the scroll, and to open its seals; for You were slain, and have redeemed us to God by Your blood out of every tribe and tongue and people and nation, [10]And have made us kings and priests to our God; and we shall reign on the earth." [11]Then I looked, and I heard the voice of

many angels around the throne, the living creatures, and the elders; and the number of them was ten thousand times ten thousand, and thousands of thousands, ¹²saying with a loud voice: "Worthy is the Lamb who was slain to receive power and riches and wisdom, and strength and honour and glory and blessing!" ¹³And every creature which is in heaven and on the earth and under the earth and such as are in the sea, and all that are in them, I heard saying: "Blessing and honour and glory and power be to Him who sits on the throne, and to the Lamb, forever and ever!" ¹⁴Then the four living creatures said, "Amen!" And the twenty-four elders fell down and worshipped Him who lives forever and ever.

Verse 1: This verse tells us that as John looked he saw within the hand of God a scroll, double-sided, with writing on both sides and sealed with seven seals. (Daniel 12:4)

Verse 2: A strong angel appeared, crying out for someone worthy enough to come to open the seals.

Verse 3: However, as far as John could tell, there was no one.

Verse 4: Thus it was that John wept, because there was no one sufficiently worthy.

Verse 5: But then, in this verse, we learn that One who was worthy had been found because one of the elders said to John, *'Behold, the Lion of the tribe of Judah'*, the One who had prevailed and who was qualified to open the seals. (Isaiah 11:10)

Verse 6: Now, as John looked, all he could see was a Lamb, a Lamb with the appearance of having been slain, as if now in the very act of being made an offering. This is very significant, for so important was the sacrificial offering of Yeshua in the sight of God that He is still represented as being in the very act of pouring out his life-blood for men's offences. This gives great benefit to our faith, for when souls come to the throne of grace they find a sacrifice prepared for them to offer to God. This shows us the two-fold nature of Yeshua the Messiah. When He came the first time He came as the Lamb of the sacrifice – and that's how John saw Him because that's how he knew Him. But the angel reveals Him as He will be when He comes again. His role as a Lamb was completed and totally fulfilled at Calvary, and when next we see Him it will be as a Lion who will tear, destroy and devour all the works of the enemy in His judgement.

We are then told that the Lamb had seven horns and seven eyes. The seven horns speak of absolute authority, power and might, while the seven eyes speak of omniscience and omnipotence, watchfulness and dynamic activity, and that together they signify the seven spirits of God, representing the Holy Spirit in His sevenfold perfection, all as belonging to and emanating from the Redeemer, the Messiah. (Zechariah 3:8-9)

Verse 7: The scroll was in the right hand of the One sitting on the throne, and the Lamb took it. Many are the discussions as to how a Lamb could take the scroll, but that is not important. What is important is that Yeshua, the Lamb of God, did take it. Interestingly there is no indication that the scroll was opened or that any of its contents were read. There was only One who was worthy to take the scroll, the Son of God and Son of Man, the One who alone has the authority to destroy Satan's kingdom, who died for the sins of all humanity, but was resurrected to rule over all creation. His death has provided for all mankind the way of salvation, but most reject it and so are worthy of judgement, not the judgement of works, as that is for the believer, but the judgement of sin and unbelief for which there is only one penalty. And the One who is worthy to open the seals is the One who is worthy to exercise that judgement.

Verse 8: Moving on we find now the worship offered to the Lamb, beginning with the four living creatures, the *seraphim*, and the twenty-four elders with their harps and golden bowls of incense containing, it says, the prayers of the saints. (Psalm 111:2)

Verses 9: Together they sang a new song, and John has recorded the words for us. Yeshua was worthy to take the scroll and to open its seals, having died for the sins of the world, enabling all who will to be redeemed (bought back) through the price of His shed blood. (Psalm 40:3)

Verse 10: And we, Jew and Gentile believers as representing the redeemed, will hold positions of authority in the coming kingdom, ruling and reigning under the King, and will function as priests in sacrificial duties. This does not mean the Mosaic sacrifices, but always presenting the fact that Yeshua's death was the one sacrifice for the many. (Exodus 19:6)

Verse 11: John looked, and obviously saw the host of angels who were singing, with the *seraphim* and the elders, all around the throne. (Daniel 7:10)

Verse 12: Seven qualities are ascribed to the Lamb in this verse, *'power and riches and wisdom, and strength and honour and glory and blessing!'* Once again we have the number seven, signifying holy completeness and total unity. In context *'riches'* are not confined to spiritual things but to all riches, earthly as well as heavenly.

Verse 13: This verse reveals that all living creatures, human and non-human, are included in praising God. This is confirmed by the fact that heaven, earth and sea are mentioned as the places where this life is found...

'in heaven' – all the angels and the glorified saints.

'on the earth' – all living humanity and the animal kingdom.

'under the earth' – these are the spirits of the dead, those in *Hades*.

'in the sea' – here speaking of all marine life.

Verse 14: The *seraphim* confirmed the praise with the word *'Amen!'* which means 'so be it' and 'trustworthy', while the twenty-four elders bowed down in adoration.

CHAPTER 6

As far as the events in heaven are concerned, the opening of the seven seals of the scroll, as described in the following chapter, begins the seven-year period popularly known as the Great Tribulation. But what about events happening on earth? From the earth's point of view there is another event and it is this that triggers this period.

Two things, then; one in heaven with the opening of the seals, but on earth something else happens. We shall discover what that is as we begin to study this event. There are various names given to this seven-year period, twenty-two of which are found in the Old Testament, nine in the New. The most common to be found in the Old Testament is 'the Day of the Lord' or, in some translations, 'the Day of Jehovah'. There is no biblical justification for naming this period 'the Great Tribulation'. This term has been adopted because of the words of Yeshua in Matthew 24:21, but where the Greek for 'tribulation' is 'tribulum', which means 'threshing instrument', an apt description for what is to happen.

The seven seals – verses 1 to 17

¹Now I saw when the Lamb opened one of the seals; and I heard one of the four living creatures saying with a voice like thunder, 'Come and see.' ²And I looked, and behold, a white horse. He who sat on it had a bow; and a crown was given to him, and he went out conquering and to conquer. ³When He opened the second seal, I heard the second living creature saying, 'Come and see.' ⁴Another horse, fiery red, went out. And it was granted to the one who sat on it to take peace from the earth, and that people should kill one another; and there was given to him a great sword. ⁵When He opened the third seal, I heard the third living creature say, 'Come and see.' So I looked, and behold, a black horse, and he who sat on it had a pair of scales in his hand. ⁶And I heard a voice in the midst of the four living creatures saying, 'A quart of wheat for a denarius, and three quarts of barley for a denarius; and do not harm the oil and the wine.' ⁷When He opened the fourth seal, I heard the voice of the fourth living creature saying, 'Come and see.' ⁸So I looked, and behold, a pale horse. And the name of him who sat on it was Death, and Hades followed with him. And power was given to them over a fourth of the earth, to kill with sword, with hunger, with death, and by the beasts of the earth. ⁹When He opened the fifth seal, I saw under the altar the souls of those who had been slain for the word of God and for the testimony which they held. ¹⁰And they cried with a loud voice, saying, 'How long, O Lord, holy and true, until You judge and avenge our blood on those who dwell on the earth?' ¹¹Then a white robe was given to each of them; and it was said to them that they should rest a little while longer, until both the number of their fellow servants and their brethren, who would be killed as they were, was completed. ¹²I looked when He opened the sixth seal, and behold, there was a great earthquake; and the sun became black as sackcloth of hair, and the moon became like blood. ¹³And the stars of heaven fell to the earth, as a fig tree drops its late figs when it is shaken by a mighty wind. ¹⁴ Then the sky receded as a scroll when it is rolled up, and every mountain and island was moved out of its place. ¹⁵And the kings of the earth, the great men, the rich men, the commanders, the mighty men, every slave and every free man, hid themselves in the caves and in the rocks of the mountains, ¹⁶and said to the mountains and rocks, 'Fall on us and hide us from the face of Him who sits on the throne and from the wrath of the Lamb! ¹⁷For the great day of His wrath has come, and who is able to stand?'

Verse 1: John now saw the Lamb holding the scroll and he watched as the first seal was opened. As the seal was broken, John heard the words of one of the *seraphim* saying, *"Come and see"*. The voice sounded like the roar of thunder, containing within it a sense of terror, judgement and majesty, and undoubtedly a voice of command. Many are the views expressed regarding the meaning here, too many for us to concern ourselves with, and it is best to interpret the words as we read them. To do otherwise would be surmise only.

Verse 2: As John looked, he saw a figure seated on a white horse. First we must establish that this figure, together with the white horse, is not the same as the figure described in chapter 19, because, in that instance, it is obviously speaking of Yeshua. We read that the crown Yeshua wears is, from the Greek, a *diadema*, which is symbolic of kingship, sovereignty and power, whereas the character we find in chapter 6 is wearing a *stephanos* crown, i.e. that of the conqueror or overcomer, and can be likened to the Greek laurel wreath.

Thus we can say that it was the opening of the first seal that revealed the Antichrist, for that is who we have here, who is now ready to come to conquer and destroy as part of his quest for world domination throughout the first half of the Tribulation period. Is he already here? Almost certainly, yes! However, as we continue we shall find that he does not gain real prominence until the second half of the Tribulation period, as we shall later discover but, nonetheless, he will begin his campaign from the opening of the first seal. From now on he will be a major character in our studies. (Zechariah 6:3)

In total there are eleven names found in the Bible that have been given to the Antichrist, and these are:

1. The seed of Satan – Genesis 3:15.

2. The little horn – Daniel 7:8.

3. The king of fierce countenance – Daniel 8:23.

4. The prince that shall come – Daniel 9:26.

5. The desolator – Daniel 9:27.

6. The wilful king – Daniel 11:36.

7. The man of sin – 2 Thessalonians 2:3.

8. The son of perdition – 2 Thessalonians 2:3.

9. The lawless one – 2 Thessalonians 2:8.

10. The Antichrist – 1 John 2:22.

11. The beast – Revelation 11:7.

Verse 3: In this verse we read of the opening of the second seal and once again we have the command *'Come and see'*, this time from a second *seraph*.

Verse 4: As this seal was opened John saw a red horse, with one seated on it whose role is to promote war. War is the opposite of peace, and so the result of the opening of the second seal is to release yet another series of wars upon the world. We shall find there are three brief world wars that will happen during the Tribulation period, and it is at this point in time that the first world war of this time begins. This is not referring to the world wars of 1914/18 or 1939/1945 but to a new war, one of three that will come in quick succession. None of these should be confused with the Gog of Magog war that must happen prior to all the events we are speaking of here, and as prophesied in Ezekiel 38 and 39, and it is only the third of these later wars that may be called the 'Armageddon Campaign'. Who are the combatants in this war of the second seal? Again there has been much debate but the most likely explanation is that it is civil war, in areas all around the world, between those who will accept the rule of the Antichrist and those who will not. (Zechariah 6:2)

Verse 5: The third seal was opened, and John heard the voice of one of the *seraphim* commanding, once more, that he should *'Come and see'*. Now he saw a black horse, where this time the rider was holding in his hand a pair of measuring scales, or balances.

Verse 6: Then there came a voice that John heard coming from an unknown source although it was probably from one of the four *seraphim*. The words spoken were: *'A quart of wheat for a denarius, and three quarts of barley for a denarius [about 5p]; and do not harm the oil and the wine.'* In the Hebrew, phrases like this identify food shortages, famine and starvation, and this is what the black horse represents. So food will be in short supply, as it so often is during and after a war, but it is significant, even with today's news, because we hear of constant threats to our food supplies, through drought, disease, and other factors. However, this verse tells us that wine and oil will not be affected, where these commodities are used in healing, and this suggests that medications will continue to be available. All this tells us of God's grace and mercy for mankind, even in judgement, but these things, too, will ultimately disappear.

Verse 7: The fourth seal was then opened and again there was the voice of a *seraphim* saying: *'Come and see.'*

Verse 8: As the seal was opened, John saw a pale horse with one sitting on it whose name was Death. Following closely behind was *Hades*, the spirit world of the dead. This does not mean that these spirits would in some way rise up to inhabit the world, but that *Hades* would rise up to engulf and hold captive its new victims. In this, the fourth judgement, 25 per cent of the world's population will perish. Death will come about through war, starvation, disease, and through attacks by wild animals. When food shortages occur, for whatever reason, it is often the animals that are the first to suffer and become desperate, and what is to happen now is that even domestic animals will hunt and kill people for food. (Jeremiah 24:10)

Verse 9: Now we have the fifth judgement being released through the opening of the fifth seal. The scene has changed and the focus is now on an altar in Paradise. Here John saw right into the spirit world, the Paradise part of *Hades*, now moved into one of the heavens following the resurrection of Yeshua. Following the Rapture, all believer saints who had been waiting in Paradise will now have direct access into the *'highest heavens'* (Deuteronomy 10:14), into the presence of God, therefore what John was seeing must have been the disembodied spirits of the martyrs who became believers during the Tribulation period, and have suffered torture and death for it. That they are now located where they are is based on the following verses in Ephesians 4:8–9:

⁸Therefore He says: 'When He ascended on high, He led captivity captive, and gave gifts to men.' ⁹ (Now this, 'He ascended' – what does it mean but that He also first descended into the lower parts of the earth?

Yeshua, after His return, will lead these victims of death and destruction out of the captivity of the new world's systems and the rule of the Antichrist, into a place of security and freedom. Evidence for what is to be is found in 2 Corinthians 12: 1–4:

¹It is doubtless not profitable for me to boast. I will come to visions and revelations of the Lord: ²I know a man in Christ who fourteen years ago – whether in the body I do not know, or whether out of the body I do not know, God knows – such a one was caught up to the third heaven. ³And I know such a man – whether in the body or out of the body I do not know, God knows – ⁴how he was caught up into Paradise and heard inexpressible words, which it is not lawful for a man to utter.

 Paradise, that place of freedom, is now in the heavenly realms, almost certainly in the third heaven referred to by Paul. Note that the direction is up; the way to *Hades* is down. It is the place where Yeshua holds the keys, the keys of death and hell. We may recall the words in Revelation 1:18:

I am He who lives, and was dead, and behold, I am alive forevermore. Amen. And I have the keys of Hades and of Death.

The altar referred to in this verse must surely be the altar of incense, the altar of prayer, and not the altar of sacrifice, the one where the blood of the sacrifice was always poured out at its foot.

Verse 10: There will be many who will suffer persecution and death for their faith, and here the victims call out to God, asking the question 'How much longer?' Just as the blood of sacrificial animals was poured out at the foot of the altar so the souls and spirits of those who die through their testimony of Yeshua during the time of the Antichrist's rule are symbolically represented as being under this altar in Paradise. One segment of theology argues that these martyrs are not part of the believing church because of their cry for vengeance, but the words are precisely the same as used by Yeshua in Luke 18:7:

> *And shall not God avenge his own elect, which cry day and night unto him, though he bear long with them?*

Verse 11: All those who have come to believe in Yeshua during these times of trouble and have died because of it are given a place in Paradise and will receive white robes, the symbol of confirmed and glorified righteousness, dressed in which they will walk and reign with Yeshua. Just when they receive these robes is not clear, but it can safely be assumed to be after the Lord's return. They are told to rest a little longer, in the blessedness in which they now exist, until such time as martyrdom ceases, but this does not mean they should stop crying out for God to avenge them.

Their being in this place raises two questions:

1. How were they saved, in the circumstances existing, and...

2. Who killed them?

The answer to the first question will be found in chapter 7, where we shall see it is the ongoing work of the 144,000 Jewish evangelists, but we must wait a little longer, until we reach chapter 17, for the answer to the second question.

Verse 12: Now we come to the opening of the sixth seal. The result of this opening will be natural convulsions, earthquakes, tsunamis, hurricane winds, every form of natural disaster, and a virtual blackout. This is the second blackout that occurs around this time, the first blackout coming before the start of the Tribulation period, while the second will be during the first half. The reference to the moon becoming the colour of blood is very significant for the Jewish people. Many times through the centuries this phenomenon has occurred at the time of a Jewish feast. Whether that is significant in the context of this verse is debatable. However, these signs are seen by many as confirmation that we are on the verge of the Messiah's return. (Joel 2:10)

Verse 13: John's vision of the stars falling from heaven is probably his way of saying that he saw the earth being bombarded with showers of substantial meteorites, just as winter figs fall from the trees in a strong wind. We may assume that these will not be tiny pebbles but will be large, sometimes very large, pieces of cosmic rock that will almost certainly cause death and destruction. (Isaiah 34:4)

Verse 14: Here we learn that the sky will be rolled up like a scroll. In this context the 'sky' is speaking of the visible heavens, the sun, moon and stars, but just what this means has not been explained by the leading theologians. It may be that it relates to the blackout mentioned a moment ago. Perhaps it helps our imagination if we think of a tightly rolled scroll, say of wallpaper, that has been unrolled but when suddenly released will roll itself up again – but what is left when this happens is not clear at all. We also read that the earth's foundations will be overthrown, where this means major geological upheaval and destruction, presumably in preparation for the new heavens and new earth. (Nahum 1:5)

Verse 15: Whatever will happen the result will be panic, accompanied by anarchy, as people try to flee and to hide from the wrath of God rather than turn to Him in repentance. Status, wealth and great physical strength will count as nothing, for terror will sweep the nations, and men will try to hide in holes and bunkers, all to no avail. (Isaiah 2:19)

Verse 16: But yet, at the same time, they appear to recognise that it is God, together with the Lamb, who is causing this. They realise this is God's wrath that is being poured out, but still they will not turn to Him. They call out for mountains and rocks to fall on them, to bury them and to hide them from the wrath of God that is being poured out. (Hosea 10:8)

Verse 17: This is the time when men and women everywhere will recognise these events as the time of God's wrath being poured out, and who is there who will be able to stand before the coming judge and not be condemned? No one! The many and varied attempts by some to relate all these happenings to aspects of church history are verging on the absurd. The best answer is to accept the words as they are written. (Nahum 1:6)

Thus it is that chapter 6 provides us with a detailed account of six of the seven judgements represented and collectively released by the seventh seal judgement, as we may read in chapter 8. The events described will no doubt follow each other in chronological order as we have them here. From what we learned earlier, remember that there will be other events taking place during this time – for instance, the ministry of Elijah and the division of the world into ten separate kingdoms.

CHAPTER 7

In this chapter we shall be dealing with the 144,000 Messianic Jews who will be responsible during this period of Tribulation for bringing worldwide revival. The way in which this will be brought about is described here.

The 144,000 Jewish evangelists – verses 1 to 8

¹After these things I saw four angels standing at the four corners of the earth, holding the four winds of the earth, that the wind should not blow on the earth, on the sea, or on any tree. ²Then I saw another angel ascending from the east, having the seal of the living God. And he cried with a loud voice to the four angels to whom it was granted to harm the earth and the sea, ³saying, 'Do not harm the earth, the sea, or the trees till we have sealed the servants of our God on their foreheads.' ⁴And I heard the number of those who were sealed. One hundred and forty-four thousand of all the tribes of the children of Israel were sealed: ⁵of the tribe of Judah twelve thousand were sealed; of the tribe of Reuben twelve thousand were sealed; of the tribe of Gad twelve thousand were sealed; ⁶of the tribe of Asher twelve thousand were sealed; of the tribe of Naphtali twelve thousand were sealed; of the tribe of Manasseh twelve thousand were sealed; ⁷of the tribe of Simeon twelve thousand were sealed; of the tribe of Levi twelve thousand were sealed; of the tribe of Issachar twelve thousand were sealed; ⁸of the tribe of Zebulun twelve thousand were sealed;

of the tribe of Joseph twelve thousand were sealed; of the tribe of Benjamin twelve thousand were sealed. ⁹After these things I looked, and behold, a great multitude which no one could number, of all nations, tribes, peoples, and tongues, standing before the throne and before the Lamb, clothed with white robes, with palm branches in their hands, ¹⁰and crying out with a loud voice, saying, 'Salvation belongs to our God who sits on the throne, and to the Lamb!' ¹¹All the angels stood around the throne and the elders and the four living creatures, and fell on their faces before the throne and worshipped God, ¹²saying: 'Amen! Blessing and glory and wisdom, thanksgiving and honour and power and might, Be to our God forever and ever. Amen.' ¹³Then one of the elders answered, saying to me, 'Who are these arrayed in white robes, and where did they come from?' ¹⁴And I said to him, 'Sir, you know.' So he said to me, 'These are the ones who come out of the great tribulation, and washed their robes and made them white in the blood of the Lamb. ¹⁵Therefore they are before the throne of God, and serve Him day and night in His temple. And He who sits on the throne will dwell among them. ¹⁶They shall neither hunger anymore nor thirst anymore; the sun shall not strike them, nor any heat; ¹⁷for the Lamb who is in the midst of the throne will shepherd them and lead them to living fountains of waters. And God will wipe away every tear from their eyes.'

Verse 1: The words *'After these things'* show that the events resulting from the opening of the sixth of the seal judgements, all of which are now completed, are but a foretaste of what was, and is, about to happen. In this verse, John records that he saw four holy angels that had been commissioned to temporarily hold back the judgement intended to harm the earth and the sea. (Ezekiel 7:2)

Verse 2: Then another angel appeared, rising up from the east or, perhaps, having the brightness of the sunrise and signifying new life. This is not Yeshua, nor an archangel, nor is it the Holy Spirit, it's just an angel. This fifth angel, having the seal and authority of God, has a message of importance for the first four angels. That he cried out with a loud voice is not emphasising the command but is to ensure that the message reaches to the four corners of the earth. The term *'living God'* is used here to clearly indicate that God has life, and that He gives life to those who believe.

Verse 3: This angel then sets the scene for holding back the destruction that has been determined until the 144,000 evangelists have been sealed, both for service and for their own protection. It is speculation only to wonder what is written on the *'seal'* and what it looks like, although there are some who think it must bear the sign of the cross. The majority, however, consider that it will be emblazoned with the name of God and of the Lamb, which may be possible even though the text says nothing. All this shows that speculation on what is not recorded is pointless. The *'we'* in this verse may include the four angels of verse 1, but not necessarily, as others not referred to may be included. (Ezekiel 9:4-6)

Verse 4: John now heard something, a voice perhaps, that may be of one of the angels, revealing a number – *'One hundred and forty-four thousand'* – which is twelve times twelve times 1,000. Such a number is natural and is of religious significance, designating something fixed and totally complete. The majority of commentators do not believe this to be a literal number but as meaning a full number known only to the Lord, and that may be true. There are one or two, however, who do think it to be a precise number, but such speculation is of little importance. These people, so numbered, are called *'servants of our God'*, identifying their role, but what is the purpose of their being sealed? Firstly it is that they might be exempt from the coming tribulation; by that is meant that they will not be harmed by any of the imminent troubles. The sealing will have the same effect as the blood splashed on the doors of the homes of the Israelites in Egypt, as in the Book of Exodus, and though it may not mean total freedom from all of the difficulties, it does mean they will be kept safe through the destruction soon to be released.

But who are these people? The following verses identify them as being of the tribes of Israel, and there are many who take the view that these are all Jewish believers, but there are others who consider them to be both Jews and Gentiles, for they argue that there is no good reason why they should be Jews only. But the scriptures are quite precise, for they say, in this verse, *'of all the tribes of the children of Israel'*, which leads us to the conclusion that they must be Jewish and certainly believers in Yeshua. In fact, in pointing this out so forcibly in scripture, God, who knew there would be Gentiles who would call themselves Jews, i.e. the Mormons, the Jehovah's Witnesses, not to mention the obscure and apostate beliefs of those who support Replacement Theology, is surely making this very clear. He wants to counter any such claims by emphasising the Jewishness of these people. When does the sealing take place? The most popular and most likely view is that this all takes place sometime between the Rapture and the start of the Tribulation period.

But now, in the following verses there is the naming of the tribes.

Verse 5: First is Judah, the tribe of David and of the Messiah, 12,000, then Reuben, 12,000, next Gad, 12,000.

Verse 6: In this verse we have Asher, 12,000, then Naphtali, 12,000, and Manasseh, 12,000.

Verse 7: Then, in this verse we have Simeon, 12,000, of Levi, 12,000, and Issachar, 12,000.

Verse 8: Next is Zebulun, 12,000, then Joseph, 12,000, and finally Benjamin,12,000.

Twelve tribes are named here but, from what we know, we will see that two appear to be missing – Ephraim and Dan. The tribe of Ephraim can probably be explained since Ephraim himself was one of the two sons of Joseph, and Joseph appears in verse 8 because he was one of the twelve sons of Jacob. But the tribe of Dan is missing and we are not sure why, and this leads us to ask whether we need to find out. It would all be guesswork if we tried, but that has not deterred the many theories that have been propounded by the teachers of prophecy, such as:, and

1. The Antichrist is of the tribe of Dan. But this theory can surely be discounted for the Antichrist will not be a Jew.

2. The False Prophet will come from the tribe of Dan, a theory proposed in the book *The Late Great Planet Earth* (Hal Lindsey, Zondervan, 1970). But this is assuming far too much since we have not been told and there is no evidence. But we can be very sure that the tribe of Dan has not disappeared,

for they are referred to in Ezekiel 48:1, as being included as part of the Millennial Kingdom. The warning to the student of prophecy in all of this is that it is wrong and very unwise to go beyond what is written.

3. Dan was the first tribe to fall into idolatry and became virtually extinct. This is error and is not supported by scripture.

Regardless of all this, the important thing to note from these verses is that the chosen 144,000 will take the gospel of the kingdom around the entire world, to call people to repentance and to turn to Him for salvation. Yeshua said this would happen in Matthew 24:14. This will be the fulfilment of that prophecy, and it will really bring the end into sight.

The saints of the coming Tribulation – verses 9 to 17

Verse 9: John then received a completely new vision, a vision of something much further ahead, in which he saw a great multitude of people, those who will be saved during the time of the Tribulation period, people from every nation of the world, so many of them that John was unable to count them. Each will be clothed in the white robes of salvation and will be grasping palm branches (in Hebrew, *'lulav'*), which are symbolic of the final feast, the Feast of Tabernacles and of the final ingathering following Yeshua's return. This will be the worldwide revival that so many have been talking about and waiting for. There may well be localised revivals at different times, as in the case of the Welsh and Hebridean, but these will be small in comparison with this worldwide gathering that is coming following the Rapture.

There is a question to ask here. Who are the *'great multitude which no one could number'*? The Futurist school tends to describe them as those who come, not through trials such as we might experience today but, through God's grace, out of the time of great tribulation that will come upon the world following the Rapture of the true believers. Among them will be Jews, those whose eyes have at last been opened to the truth of their Messiah, and Gentiles, some of them possibly unbelieving churchgoers who didn't qualify for the Rapture, but they and the majority who have not previously heard the gospel message will be those who respond to the truth during the Tribulation period as the result of the ministry of the 144,000. (Leviticus 23:40)

Verse 10: And this great multitude of people will join the *seraphim* and the elders worshipping around the throne and crying out, not the usual restrained murmurings of a Sunday service, but full-throated and with loud voices, saying *'Salvation belongs to our God'*. Nothing disrespectful about this at all, even if there are some who consider such crying out implies a lack of reverence towards God. The language used here reveals that all this takes place in heaven, not in some intermediate staging post, all as confirmed in chapter 20. (Psalm 3:8)

Verse 11: The scene now is one of great majesty as all the angels (the five we have already heard about – or the entire heavenly host), together with the elders and the *seraphim*, fall down on their faces to worship God.

Verse 12: In this verse we have a note of the words they speak: *'Amen! Blessing and glory and wisdom, Thanksgiving and honour and power and might, Be to our God forever and ever. Amen.'*

Verse 13: One of the elders, representing redeemed humanity, answered John's unasked question by phrasing it for him: *'Who are these arrayed in white robes, and where did they come from?'*

Verse 14: John spoke with great reverence and said that he didn't have the answer to that question but he believed the elder could tell him. The answer he had was that they were what are called 'Tribulation saints', those that had survived the Tribulation period, together with those that had not, and had just arrived at this place where John could see them. They had been raised up and had washed their robes, the filthy rags of an earthly life, and had made them white through their faith and trust in Yeshua the Messiah. This must mean they had been judged and declared righteous. (Genesis 49:11)

Verse 15: We now have the scene where the saints who have come to know Yeshua as the result of the ministry of the 144,000 are being comforted in heaven. All will have experienced violence, torture and death during the time of the Tribulation period. The saints are therefore qualified to stand before the throne of God and they will serve Him through performing any service He chooses for them. They will serve Him *'day and night'* it says, but this does not mean a twenty-four hour period, it means for all eternity. The correct interpretation of *'will dwell among them'* is *'shall spread His tabernacle over them'*, and means that He will dwell with them forever. (Leviticus 26:11)

Verse 16: The scene that is described in this verse must be the heaven of heavens. None of the experiences of the past will be repeated, no more hunger or thirst, no more of the blistering heat of the desert of God's wrath. The scene described here is beyond our imagining. Looking at the world scene today, with natural disasters increasing and intensifying, plus political unrest in many parts of the world, with wars, massacres and death, it's hard to think that things can get much worse. There is famine, sickness and disease with the concern that antibiotics are losing their effectiveness. Fear of the unknown, too. Oh, yes, it will get worse, without a doubt. (Isaiah 49:10)

Verse 17: But then the elder spoke encouraging words to John, for the Lamb, standing in the central point before God's throne, would be their shepherd, leading them to fountains of living water. It will be with many tears that these saints will come out of the Tribulation period, but when they have overcome, it will be God Himself who will wipe their tears away. From these verses we cannot be sure whether the events from verse 9 onwards occur immediately before or just after the Second Coming of Yeshua, but with the scene set as being before the throne that we read of in chapter 4, we can surely accept that it must be before. (Ezekiel 34:23)

CHAPTER 8

We can now move on to study chapters 8 and 9 of this book, and to the second series of judgements – the first of which will be the trumpet judgements, following which we shall come to the mid-point of the Tribulation period. You will probably remember that chapter 5 was a prelude to chapter 6; now, in the same way, verses 1 to 6 of this chapter are a prelude to other events that are to follow. Remember that what John is seeing are symbolic images, not reality but primarily communicating to us the effects of what he is seeing.

The opening of the seventh seal –
verses 1 to 6

¹When He opened the seventh seal, there was silence in heaven for about half an hour. ²And I saw the seven angels who stand before God, and to them were given seven trumpets. ³Then another angel, having a golden censer, came and stood at the altar. He was given much incense, that he should offer it with the prayers of all the saints upon the golden altar which was before the throne. ⁴And the smoke of the incense, with the prayers of the saints, ascended before God from the angel's hand. ⁵Then the angel took the censer, filled it with fire from the altar, and threw it to the earth. And there were noises, thunderings, lightnings, and an earthquake. ⁶So the seven angels who had the seven trumpets prepared themselves to sound.

Verse 1: The time had come for the opening of the seventh seal and, as it was opened, we may observe the result – nothing! Nothing happened and it tells us that for a period of time of *'about half an hour'* there was silence in heaven. Does that mean that heaven was stunned into shocked silence? There is no way of telling, but perhaps it does suggest that time is actually measured in heaven. If this is so, it could put an end to the theory that time in heaven is always 'the continuous now', but it may be no more than a limitation of the language where John was trying to describe what he saw.

However, it may be that we can see this silence as the anxious anticipation of those in heaven as they wait for the contents of the seventh seal to be revealed. There are some who interpret the silence as meaning the 1,000 years of the Millennium, others that it speaks of the church's silence in prayer but, as with all these things, what isn't said is best left unsaid and the words accepted as they are written.

Verse 2: During the silence, John saw seven angels, seven particular angels because of the definite article – but not archangels nor the seven spirits of God – which had been selected from the myriads to blow the seven trumpets.

Verse 3: Then another angel appeared, just an ordinary one, but real with no special qualities despite the fanciful imaginations of some theologians. He held a golden censer and moved to stand by the side of the golden altar. But which altar is it, the altar of incense or the altar of sacrifice? Almost certainly it is the altar spoken of earlier, in chapter 6, verse 9, the altar of incense. He is given much incense which is to be blended with the prayers of the saints, making them more effective as a sweet-smelling savour to God. The interpretation of this seems to mean that the trumpet judgements that are about to follow are God's answer to the prayers of the Tribulation saints who are now in Paradise. (Psalm 141:2-3)

Verse 4: The whole imagery of this verse suggests that the prayers of the saints on earth are blended simultaneously with the incense released by the angel, and that God will be gracious and will hear the prayers during the trials of the Tribulation period. The trials will be the natural result of the judgements that are to be released through the blowing of the trumpets.

Verse 5: Here it would seem that the angel with the censer must have scattered its contents somewhere for he then filled it with fire from the altar and threw the fire down onto the earth. This tells us that the answer to the prayers of the saints was about to descend upon the earth, for the fire is the sign of God's judgements upon an ungodly world. The result of the fire will be '*noises, thunderings, lightnings, and an earthquake*'. (Ezekiel 10:2)

Verse 6: And now all seven of the angels with the trumpets prepare to blow them. (Exodus 18:6)

The trumpets are sounded – verses 7 to 13

It is thought by some of the Futurist School that the trumpet judgements that follow are revealing in more detail the terrors that are to come upon the earth, culminating with the destruction of the Antichrist. In other words, the trumpet judgements are an introduction to that part of the Tribulation period existing during the years or months immediately preceding the appearance of the Messiah in clouds of glory, and this is an acceptable interpretation.

> *[7]The first angel sounded: and hail and fire followed, mingled with blood, and they were thrown to the earth. And a third of the trees were burned up, and all green grass was burned up. [8]Then the second angel sounded: and something like a great mountain burning with fire was thrown into the sea, and a third of the sea became blood. [9]And a third of the living creatures in the sea died, and a third of the ships were destroyed. [10]Then the third angel sounded: and a great star fell from heaven, burning like a torch, and it fell on a third of the rivers and on the springs of water. [11]The name of the star is Wormwood. A third of the waters became wormwood, and many men died from the water, because it was made bitter. [12]Then the fourth angel sounded: And a third of the sun was struck, a third of the moon, and a third of the stars, so that a third of them were darkened. A third of the day did not shine, and likewise the night. [13]And I looked, and I heard an angel flying through the midst of heaven, saying with a loud voice, 'Woe, woe, woe to the inhabitants*

of the earth, because of the remaining blasts of the trumpet of the three angels who are about to sound!'

Verse 7: The first angel blew and the first trumpet judgement was now released. For John the result was that he saw what appeared to be hail, fire and blood being thrown down upon the earth where the result was that *'a third of the trees were burned up and all the green grass was burned up.'* There are many interpretations as to what this means from this world's perspective but, taken literally, as it should be, it means that one third of the earth's surface will be destroyed. The suggestion that the subject here is Israel, where the trees identify the Jewish leadership and the grass represents the ordinary Jewish people, is pushing allegory a good bit too far. However, by the time we get around to the end of the Tribulation period, and the return of the Messiah, there is going to be very little of the world as we know it left that will be habitable. (Isaiah 28:2)

Verse 8: Then the second angel blew his trumpet. The imaginations begin to run a bit wild among some of the experts at this point, those who try to connect future events with historical invasions of the lands around the Mediterranean Sea. But there are those who believe it better to accept the text as it is written and to interpret the words on the basis of established understanding. For instance, the sea in this verse typically means the nations of the world; the great mountain could mean a large meteorite or possibly an underwater volcanic eruption, the sea becoming polluted as a result, and having the appearance or consistency of blood. (Exodus 7:17)

Verse 9: The consequence of this activity appeared to be the destruction of one third of all marine life, and the loss of one third of all shipping. What we can say for sure here is that these verses indicate some catastrophic happenings on the earth, affecting millions of people, and are in very close conjunction with the return of the Messiah who will, on His return, immediately destroy the Antichrist.

Verse 10: Then the third angel blew his trumpet and a *'great star'* fell from heaven. Studying the opinions of many theologians, we realise how varied and arbitrary are their interpretations and how hopeless is the task of ever trying to solve the mysteries from their perspective.

Some say the *'great star'* was Satan, or Attila the Hun, or the Antichrist, or they link it to the growth of the apostate church. Imaginative, to say the least! Accurate? Probably not! Perhaps more logical, but still speculative, is that it could be some nuclear catastrophe, such as Chernobyl, which polluted many waters. (Isaiah 14:12)

Verse 11: The name of the star is *'Wormwood'* which, in Greek, is *'absinthe'* and it created a bitter taste. Whatever the star is, its effect is that one third of all drinking water will be polluted and many will die from drinking it. Some compare this pollution to the *'waters of Marah'* as in Exodus 15:23–25, but now there is no healing for those who drink this water. (Jeremiah 9:15)

Verse 12: The trumpet of the fourth judgement was then blown by the fourth angel. The result of this was that one third of the world's natural light source was destroyed. This can be taken in two ways, but there is not enough evidence in the text for us to be absolutely clear. For instance...

- Will one third of all light from sun, moon and stars be destroyed in some way?

- Or will one third of the light from these heavenly bodies be prevented from reaching the earth's surface, with smoke or volcanic dust being possibilities?

Either way, the effect will be quite disastrous. (Isaiah 13:10)

Verse 13: This verse tells of an eagle or, as some translations have it, an angel, which is probably the correct interpretation, *flying through the midst of heaven, saying in a loud voice, "Woe, woe, woe..."'* Some have seen the eagle as representative of the Roman Empire, others suggest it is the voice of eminent teachers in the church, or some prophet to be expected at these times. Others think it could be the Messiah Himself. As someone once said, 'Is it any wonder that men regard this book as an enigma with such interpretations as guides'.[3] Leaving all that to one side, has not all that has gone before not been quite bad enough? Well, it is now going to get a great deal worse, for we are told that the next three trumpet blasts are going to release woe upon woe. Thus we

---

3   Weidner.

can describe the fifth, sixth and seventh trumpet judgements as 'woe' judgements in that they will begin to bring intense suffering directly upon the people. Both the first and second 'woe' judgements reveal that there will be a sharp increase in satanic activity in the world and then, after an interlude, will come the third 'woe', which is the seventh trumpet, heralding the introduction of the seven 'bowl' judgements.

CHAPTER 9

This chapter deals with the first of the two 'woe' judgements, beginning with the blowing of the fifth and sixth trumpets...

The first two woes – verses 1 to 21

¹Then the fifth angel sounded: And I saw a star fallen from heaven to the earth. To him was given the key to the bottomless pit. ²And he opened the bottomless pit, and smoke arose out of the pit like the smoke of a great furnace. So the sun and the air were darkened because of the smoke of the pit. ³Then out of the smoke locusts came upon the earth. And to them was given power, as the scorpions of the earth have power. ⁴They were commanded not to harm the grass of the earth, or any green thing, or any tree, but only those men who do not have the seal of God on their foreheads. ⁵And they were not given authority to kill them, but to torment them for five months. Their torment was like the torment of a scorpion when it strikes a man. ⁶In those days men will seek death and will not find it; they will desire to die, and death will flee from them. ⁷The shape of the locusts was like horses prepared for battle. On their heads were crowns of something like gold, and their faces were like the faces of men. ⁸They had hair like women's hair, and their teeth were like lions' teeth. ⁹And they had breastplates like breastplates of iron, and the sound of their wings was like the sound of chariots with many horses running into battle. ¹⁰They had tails like scorpions, and there were stings in their tails. Their power was to hurt men five months. ¹¹And they had as king over them the angel of the bottomless pit, whose name in Hebrew is Abaddon, but in Greek he has the name Apollyon. [12]One woe is past. Behold, still two more woes are coming after these things. [13]Then the sixth angel sounded: And I heard a voice from the four horns of the golden altar which is before God, [14]saying to the sixth angel who had the trumpet, 'Release the four angels who are bound at the great river Euphrates.' [15]So the four angels, who had been prepared for the hour and day and month and year, were released to kill a third of mankind. [16]Now the number of the army of the horsemen was two hundred million; I heard the number of them. [17]And thus I saw the horses in the vision: those who sat on them had breastplates of fiery red, hyacinth blue, and sulphur yellow; and the heads of the horses were like the heads of lions; and out of their mouths came fire, smoke, and brimstone. [18]By these three plagues a third of mankind was killed – by the fire and the smoke and the brimstone which came out of their mouths. [19]For their power is in their mouth and in their tails; for their tails are like serpents, having heads; and with them they do harm. [20]But the rest of mankind, who were not killed by these plagues, did not repent of the works of their hands, that they should not worship demons, and idols of gold, silver, brass, stone, and wood, which can neither see nor hear nor walk. [21]And they did not repent of their murders or their sorceries or their sexual immorality or their thefts.

Verse 1: The fifth angel now blew his trumpet and, even as it sounded, John records how he saw another star or, more correctly, an angel that had fallen to the earth, not descended as might have been expected. We cannot identify this angel but since 'star' identifies one of God's angelic agents, we can be fairly certain that it was good one, and he does have a key to the abyss, the bottomless pit, which has the meaning 'unseen world'. Some say this was Satan himself, based on Isaiah 14:12 and Luke 10:18, but this is not acceptable. Just when this angel fell we are not told, just that John saw it after it arrived. (Isaiah 14:13-14)

Verse 2: This same angel was seen to use his key to open the entrance to the abyss and great clouds of smoke, as of a great furnace, billowed out. So thick was the smoke that it blacked out the sun and the atmosphere around. This is the third blackout. To John, as he looked, the abyss in his vision appears to be somewhere deep underground, having a shaft leading to it and having a cover over it that is normally kept locked. We won't go into any more detail here, but briefly there are three conclusions that can be made:

- The direction to it is always downward.

- It is never associated with human beings, with the exception of the Antichrist, and is always the place of the fallen angels.

- The abyss is one compartment of *Sheol* and *Hades* intended for the temporary confinement of fallen angels, but these will be released through the blowing of the fifth trumpet. (Genesis 19:28)

Verse 3: But that was not all, for along with the smoke came what appeared to John to be many locusts, with the poison power of scorpions. These are not real insects, of course but, once again using biblical analogy, we know that scorpions symbolically identify demonic beings, so that what is happening here is a release of more satanically inspired evil spirits upon the earth to reinforce the evil already here. The suggestion by some that these locusts are actually helicopters is pushing credibility a bit too far. (Exodus 10:12-15)

Verse 4: The purpose of this invasion is not to harm what is left of the vegetation of the natural world, as locusts would, but it is to torment men and women, all those who do not have God's seal on their foreheads, meaning, amongst others, the 144,000. This fixes the timing of this invasion as being after their being sealed, as we read in chapter 7. This plague is not selective, as some say, falling only on the unbelieving Jews, for the text does not say that. No, this plague will affect all humanity. It's as we observe the situation in the world as it is today we see all the words of Yeshua in Matthew 24 coming increasingly true, but what we may understand from this verse is that things will become infinitely worse. There will be wars, pestilence, famine, murder, as well as natural disasters.

Verse 5: This torment is to last for five months which, as it happens, is ordinarily the time taken by real locusts as they ravage the countryside. The sting of these demonic beings is like the sting of the scorpion, it says, but whether this is intended in a literal sense is not clear. What we can determine is that the effect on people will be to cause torment – probably physical, mental and emotional.

Verse 6: What is clear is that the effect is one of overwhelming pain such that, as it says in this verse, men and women will seek death because of it, but they will not be able to find it. They will wish for death, rather than choose life through repentance, but attempts at suicide will not succeed and they will have to go through the whole five months of suffering. (Job 3:21)

Verse 7: John sees these locusts as though they were warhorses, with protective armour and with crowns that looked a bit like gold. The faces of these insects had the appearance of men's faces, but note that all the descriptions in this verse tell us that the features only resembled how they are described. These are not real creatures, of course, but are merely images intended to communicate to us the effects of the judgements coming upon the earth. This is confirmed by John's descriptions, that these beings were *'like'* something natural

Verse 8: Again, in this verse, we note that the description of the *'locusts'* as having hair *'like'* women's hair and teeth *'like'* lion's teeth indicates that what John saw only resembled the real thing, and he describes things the best way he can. It seems certain that the reasons behind the visions are not that there should be a focus on their appearance, but far more on their purpose and effect. (Joel 1:6)

Verse 9: In this verse we read that John saw the breasts of all these insects as being protected with what appeared to be plates of iron, and also that the noise of their wings as they flew was like the sound of galloping horses pulling chariots. (Joel 2:5)

Verse 10: Again, the description of locusts having tails *'like'* scorpion's tails shows us that there is nothing of natural origin here, for locusts don't have tails. These tails appear to contain stings that can cause pain, and they use them to hurt people for the five months of this plague. Trying to envisage what this all means is not easy. Is the hurt physical? Or is it the damage done to the souls and spirits of men through the evil being released? It could be any or all of these things.

Verse 11: These beings have as their head, or leader, one who is named, in Hebrew, *Abaddon* and in Greek *Apollyon*, which name in both languages means 'Destroyer' or 'Destruction'. In some Bible versions this leader has the title *'angel of the abyss'* which could suggest this is not Satan, but the names here confirm that it is. This 'angel' is the personification of the place from which he has come; to Jewish understanding this is the lowest place in hell, the place of utter corruption and destruction, and such a description just about sums this being up. But what do the theologians say about this?

Some argue that the locusts represent the Roman invasion of Judaea and that the fallen star was Nero. Others say that they are the heretics, the Zealots, who raged against the Orthodox during the Jewish civil war. Still others say they are the Islamic armies of the Saracens out of Arabia. None of these arguments, and there are others, address the fact that the 'woe' trumpets are sounded at the *'time of the end'* (referred to in the Book of Daniel), and therefore still future, and that events of 1,000 years ago cannot possibly be the fulfilment of this prophetic vision. (Job 28:22, 31:12)

Verse 12: Going on, in this verse we might reasonably think that it's time for things to get better for now, after five months of intense suffering, the first 'woe' is past – but none should hold their breath for there are two more 'woes' still to come.

Verse 13: And so, in this verse, the sixth angel blew his trumpet and with it the second 'woe' was released upon the earth. It seems that a voice proceeded out of the horns of the altar itself, the altar which is before God, a statement best accepted as it is written rather than to try to disseminate any other meaning.

Verse 14: This voice, from someone unknown, is addressed to the sixth angel, where the command that is issued is in answer to the prayers of the saints, those who are under the altar and who are calling for vengeance for their blood shed upon it. The call is to release the four fallen angels who have been held bound on the banks of the River Euphrates. Some say these are good angels, but this is hard to reconcile in the light of where they have been and are about to do. The river here can be identified with the place from where all the punishments that affected Israel in the past have originated. However, although the locust army must be taken as mystical, the river should not. It's real. (Genesis 15:18)

Verse 15: That these four angels were evil is clear from the fact they had been held bound, but now they were to be released. Who is to release them is not made clear, for the sixth angel simply issued the commandment, but the 'who' is of no real consequence; it is the 'why' that is important. They have been held bound for a time determined by God, but now they are to be released for a specific end-time task – to kill a third of all mankind!

Verse 16: We have just been told of one demonic invasion, but now we have another one, in far greater numbers and with evil of much worse intensity. These four evil angels have waited a long time for this moment, but now they have been set free to come out and kill. But who or what are they, and what do they represent? There are some who say this prophecy was fulfilled by Titus against Jerusalem in 70AD, others that this refers to the Turkman invasion that broke up the Greek Empire years later, around 1055AD. Still others argue that this future invasion is of human origin, and remember that Chairman Mao of China once said he could field an army of 200 million men. The belief that this invasion will be by China is pure fantasy for, in the context, this is not possible. Note that this invasion is different from the earlier one during the time of the first woe, for here John was seeing horses and horsemen, not locusts. But what was the source of the voice that told John the number of this invasion? We are not told and it probably doesn't matter.

Verse 17: John now tells us that he clearly saw the horses and their riders in the vision. Look at the description of the breastplates and also consider the fire, smoke and brimstone. Where brimstone is found in scripture it is associated with hell or the burning judgements of God. There is little doubt, therefore, that this is not describing a literal army of men and horses but is speaking of a wave of demonic evil bringing unspeakable horror. The very imaginative interpretation of the words '*out of their mouths came fire,* *smoke, and brimstone'* as being descriptive of the cannons used by the Turks against Constantinople in 1453 A.D. cannot be seriously considered.

Verse 18: *'By these three plagues'* said John, but what was he speaking of here? The word *'plagues'* does not appear in the Greek text but three 'somethings' are implied. Is it something to do with the fire, the smoke and the brimstone, or does it relate to three physical conditions that will exist in the latter days? It doesn't say and nobody knows, so attempting to offer a positive answer could be confusing. What we do know is that the effect will be to kill one third of all mankind. Just as one third of all vegetation, ships and fish had earlier been destroyed, now one third of all the people of the world are to perish. What will be the nature of their deaths? It will be through demonically inspired torture and executions of large parts of the population, Jews and Gentiles alike, as the evil spirits, seen as locusts and horses, work their evil spells in the hearts of those bearing the mark of the Antichrist.

Verse 19: This verse has created some very strange interpretations, and not surprising, for how can it be explained? The reference to *'mouth'* may link them to the source of the fire, the smoke and the brimstone, but that is in no way certain. A possible answer may be that *'mouth'* is a way of describing the accusing lies of those who denounce their fellow citizens. In addition there is the description of the horses' tails being like serpents having heads and, with them, doing great harm. None of this can be explained logically. The most likely answer is that these verses are totally symbolic and that the horses' mouths and the serpents' heads on their tails refer to the moral corruption and destructive powers that are spreading around the world.

Verse 20: Finally we see that despite all the horrors of this time those who survive will still not turn to God, the One who could save them from it, but they continue in their immorality, injustice, violence, the worship of Satan, and the worship of idols, by this meaning material things, wealth, status and power.

Verse 21: Neither do they show any desire to repent of murder, witchcraft, sexual perversion or robbery, so there will be worse consequences to come. But now, with the blowing of the sixth trumpet, we have reached the end of the first half of the Tribulation period and the first and second woes are past. The chronological events of the first three and a half years have been completed.

Chapter 10

It will be at this time that major changes will take place in the world's political and religious circles, and there will be twelve key things that will happen. The order in which they will occur is not clear and they may not be in the order in which we shall consider them but, no matter, we can be sure that they will happen during this mid-Tribulation period.

The mid-point of the Tribulation period – verses 1 to 11

¹I saw still another mighty angel coming down from heaven, clothed with a cloud. And a rainbow was on his head, his face was like the sun, and his feet like pillars of fire. ² He had a little book open in his hand. And he set his right foot on the sea and his left foot on the land, ³and cried with a loud voice, as when a lion roars. When he cried out, seven thunders uttered their voices. ⁴Now when the seven thunders uttered their voices, I was about to write; but I heard a voice from heaven saying to me, 'Seal up the things which the seven thunders uttered, and do not write them.' ⁵The angel whom I saw standing on the sea and on the land raised up his hand to heaven ⁶and swore by Him who lives forever and ever, who created heaven and the things that are in it, the earth and the things that are in it, and the sea and the things that are in it, that there should be delay no longer, ⁷but in the days of the sounding of the seventh angel, when he is about to sound, the mystery of God would be finished, as He declared to His servants the prophets. ⁸Then the voice which I heard from heaven spoke to me again and said, 'Go, take the little book which is open in the hand of the angel who stands on the sea and on the earth.' ⁹So I went to the angel and said to him, 'Give me the little book.' And he said to me, 'Take and eat it; and it will make your stomach bitter, but it will be as sweet as honey in your mouth.' ¹⁰Then I took the little book out of the angel's hand and ate it, and it was as sweet as honey in my mouth. But when I had eaten it, my stomach became bitter. ¹¹And he said to me, 'You must prophesy again about many peoples, nations, tongues, and kings.'

The scroll

Verse 1: In this verse John saw another strong angel in his vision, this one holding a little book, or scroll. What do we know about this individual? There isn't much to go on but many would argue, perhaps with good reason, that this angel is none other than Yeshua Himself because of the description – the rainbow, the shining face and the feet like pillars of fire. But John, who has been so precise in his descriptions where Yeshua has been concerned, and when he did see Him he said so, describes this being as an angel, so it is almost certainly as John said. That he is a messenger from the Messiah is clear and, being clothed with cloud, is a messenger of divine judgement. Regarding the 'rainbow', the word here should be prefaced with the definite article indicating that it is not an ordinary one. This rainbow is the rainbow of the Noahic Covenant and is the emblem of God's covenant mercy. (Ezekiel 1:26-28)

Verse 2: It tells us that this new angel had a *'little book open in his hand'*, which raises two questions. What is meant by little? And is it a book or a scroll? It may be little when compared to the book in chapter 5, or it may be little because John had to eat it, and it seems that it is a book because it is open in the angel's hand, and a scroll would need two hands. However, in the original text it is described as a scroll, but that is all speculative and of no real importance. This angel stands with one foot on the sea and one on the land which, for want of a better explanation, would seem to represent the scope, glory and majesty of the Messiah, whose messenger this angel is. Sea and land, in this instance, should be taken as literal, both claimed by the Messiah as being His and indicating that God's authority and judgement extends over the whole earth.

Verse 3: It tells us here that the angel cried out with a roar like a lion's, but the words used, if any, were not recorded. The significance here is almost certainly the threatening nature of what was to be revealed. The roar was accompanied by the sound of seven thunders, but there is no explanation as to their meaning. Because of the definite article, and in line with previous symbolism, these thunders are actual entities, just as the seven churches, the seven seals, etc., but just what that means to us is unclear.

Verse 4: But for some reason or other, not disclosed here, John was forbidden to write down the meaning of these thunders. He was told to seal them up, in other words he was not to record what he had heard. The meaning is obviously intended to be kept secret, revealed to John alone. That, of course, has not prevented people going into all sorts of theological gymnastics in order to create a meaning. Some say the entire account is a prelude to the destruction of Jerusalem. Others believe the text is describing the Reformation and Martin Luther, and that the *'little book'* is the Bible. Yet others say that the book was little because it only contained a small portion of God's purposes, and it was open because God was about to disclose its contents. However, God intended the contents to be kept secret and that should be good enough for us. We must wait until the time is right for us to know. (Daniel 8:26)

Verses 5–7: In these verses an announcement is made by the angel who stood on the sea and on the land and who swore by the Creator of all things, that speaks of the imminent conclusion of the purposes of God. The result of the soon blowing of the seventh trumpet will be that the mystery of God will be complete. The *'mystery'* has a number of facets, i.e., God's scheme of redemption for mankind, the destiny of the world, and the completion of the Eternal Kingdom. All this is because the seventh trumpet is about to be sounded and the last series of judgements, the bowl judgements, are soon to be released, following which the wrath of God will be finished and the reign of Yeshua and His saints will begin. (Daniel 12:7; Amos 3:7)

Verse 8: John heard the voice again, and this time he was told to go to the angel who stood on the sea and the land and to take the little book from him.

Verse 9: Where is John at this moment? Is he still in heaven? Or has he switched positions so that he is now on the earth? He was near enough to the angel to take the book and, as he took it, the angel told him to eat it. He was warned that, in doing so, he would find it both bitter and sweet. (Jeremiah 15:16)

Verse 10: To eat it is a way of saying that he was to take its contents right into his innermost parts, into his heart and understanding. The sweetness and the bitterness are not two separate experiences but are the constituents of the whole – the sweetness is the compliance with God's will, the bitterness the awareness of the awesomeness of the final judgements to be released upon the whole world.

Verse 11: Now the command was to go and prophesy again. This was a direct command from God, it was not something laid upon him because he ate the book. What he was to prophesy was what he would find in the little book, the book that relates to the fulfilment of the mysteries and purposes of God. The recipients of the message of the little book are all the inhabitants of the earth, for it is to them that the message is sent. (Ezekiel 37:4, 9)

What we, as believers, can draw from this is that if the study of the 'end times' remains as nothing more than 'sweetness' in our memories, it has failed to do its job. It means that we are not digesting the word in full, for if we do, it will certainly result in a bitter taste. If we believe that the horrors of the Tribulation period will be as we have been told, we should be driven into reaching out to all mankind – to Jew and to Gentile, to family, friends and strangers alike. There is only one way any of us can escape this time, and that is through a new birth and by accepting Yeshua as Lord, confessing His life, death, resurrection and ascension as truth, and to do that sooner rather than later. Only the true believers will experience the Rapture, and only the raptured will escape

God's wrath. Thus the Rapture is the hope of the church, the 'invisible' church, and escape via the Rapture is the only way to avoid the coming time of Tribulation. If this is true, we should be inspired to reach out to the unbelievers, knowing what is coming, and by persuasive argument convince them of their need of salvation because, if they don't accept it from us, they may not accept it from the 144,000 evangelists. So we have an obligation to all, for the consequences of the rejection of Yeshua as the Messiah of Israel do not bear thinking about.

CHAPTER 11

The two witnesses – verses 1 to 19

As we now turn our attention to chapter 11, we shall find two more events that must happen by the time the mid-Tribulation period is reached. It is in this chapter that we may understand something of the content of the scroll as John was told, in the previous chapter, to '*prophesy again*'. This means that he must repeat prophecies already given but not so far fulfilled, in fact it will be all those relating to the mid- to end-Tribulation events. So, just as John had declared the first prophecies, so now he must proclaim again the same events but in more detail, in the following chapters. This prophecy is hard to understand except in the light of what is to follow.

> *¹Then I was given a reed like a measuring rod. And the angel stood, saying, 'Rise and measure the temple of God, the altar, and those who worship there. ²But leave out the court which is outside the temple, and do not measure it, for it has been given to the Gentiles. And they will tread the holy city underfoot for forty-two months. ³And I will give power to my two witnesses, and they will prophesy one thousand two hundred and sixty days, clothed in sackcloth.' ⁴These are the two olive trees and the two lampstands standing before the God of the earth. ⁵And if anyone wants to harm them, fire proceeds from their mouth and devours their enemies. And if anyone wants to harm them, he must be killed in this manner. ⁶These have power to shut heaven, so that no rain falls in the days of their prophecy; and they have power over waters to turn them to blood, and to strike*

the earth with all plagues, as often as they desire. ⁷When they finish their testimony, the beast that ascends out of the bottomless pit will make war against them, overcome them, and kill them. ⁸And their dead bodies will lie in the street of the great city which spiritually is called Sodom and Egypt, where also our Lord was crucified. ⁹Then those from the peoples, tribes, tongues, and nations will see their dead bodies three-and-a-half days, and not allow their dead bodies to be put into graves. ¹⁰And those who dwell on the earth will rejoice over them, make merry, and send gifts to one another, because these two prophets tormented those who dwell on the earth. ¹¹Now after the three-and-a-half days the breath of life from God entered them, and they stood on their feet, and great fear fell on those who saw them. ¹²And they heard a loud voice from heaven saying to them, 'Come up here.' And they ascended to heaven in a cloud, and their enemies saw them. ¹³In the same hour there was a great earthquake, and a tenth of the city fell. In the earthquake seven thousand people were killed, and the rest were afraid and gave glory to the God of heaven. ¹⁴The second woe is past. Behold, the third woe is coming quickly. ¹⁵Then the seventh angel sounded: And there were loud voices in heaven, saying, 'The kingdoms of this world have become the kingdoms of our Lord and of His Christ, and He shall reign forever and ever!' ¹⁶And the twenty-four elders who sat before God on their thrones fell on their faces and worshipped God, ¹⁷saying: 'We give You thanks, O Lord God Almighty, the One who is and who was and who is to come, because You have taken Your great power and reigned. ¹⁸The nations were angry, and Your wrath has come, and the time of the dead, that they should be judged, and that You should reward Your servants the prophets and the saints, and those who fear Your name, small and great, and should destroy those who destroy the earth.' ¹⁹Then the temple of God was opened in heaven, and the ark of His covenant was seen in His temple. And there were lightnings, noises, thunderings, an earthquake, and great hail.

Verses 1 & 2: In these two verses we have a mysterious episode concerning a reed that had the appearance of a measuring rod. This reed was placed in John's hand but there is no clear indication as to who gave it to him. There is little to cause us to doubt that John is here speaking about true believers, identified as '*the temple of God, the altar, and those who worship there*', and unbelievers, which are typified in these verses by *'the court which is outside the temple'*. We should also take literally the period of *'forty-two months'* as meaning the three and a half years of the second half of the Tribulation. The most probable interpretation of this is that the temple will have been rebuilt by this time and that the measuring implies both the precise proportions of the restored temple and also the strict number of Jewish and Gentile believers. The sanctuary, therefore, portrays the true believers who refuse the claims of the Antichrist, while the others in the outer court are the wicked who will submit to those claims and will accept the mark of the beast.

As we have so often found, there are a number of views as to what these periods of time represent. One view is that, symbolically, they represent the *'times of the Gentiles'*, (Luke 21:24), either from the dates of the Babylonian exile or from the destruction of Jerusalem by the Romans under Titus, continuing to the Second Coming of the Messiah. Another, and quite popular view, is that each of the 1,260 days represents a year, 1,260 years. The problem is that none of those supporting this idea can agree a starting point. The third, and most logical, view is that it is taken literally and is referring to the second half of Daniel's seventieth week, the days of the Antichrist's reign. We can safely discount the thought that this is speaking of the Reformation, and the authority of Luther as proposed by some. Likewise we can reject the idea that the temple and its surroundings has somehow become the church, as suggested by others. (Zechariah 2:1-2)

Verse 3: God says He will give power to His two witnesses. That He does do that is confirmed by the miracles these two perform. We note that their ministry will last for 1,260 days, or three and a half years, which means they must have been ministering throughout the whole of the first half of the Tribulation. That they are described as His witnesses tells us that He knows them and trusts them.

Verse 4: In this verse the two witnesses are described as being the two olive trees and the two candlesticks standing before the Lord. Why olive trees? Probably because the anointing and power of the Holy Spirit rests on them, but suggestions such as their representing the Law and Israel are among many others. What may be the correct understanding is down to individual interpretation. (Zechariah 4:14)

Zechariah, in his vision, saw what John was seeing and asked a question that doesn't really get a proper answer. He is only told that they are *'the two anointed ones'*. But who are they? Can we find out? We know they are given power and authority to prophesy, and it is possible that John, in his narrative, recognised them. As is usual in these things, there are numerous candidates put forward by those who attempt to identify them from among the people of the past, for instance Elijah, Moses, Enoch, etc. Some say:

- They must be Elijah and Enoch since they didn't die, and it is appointed that all men must die, therefore these two must be the ones who return to earth, to complete their business and then to die. But if this theory is true, what about all the believers who have been raptured? Do they have to come back to complete their lives on earth so that they can also die physically?

- Another idea is that the two must be Elijah and Moses, because they were the ones who appeared with Yeshua on the Mount of Transfiguration. There is, of course, no way of proving this theory.

- They are Elijah and Moses, but for another reason, say others, which was because neither was able to complete their ministry, so it has to be them who must come back to finish off. But who said their ministries were incomplete? Surely God decides that.

- Yes, they are Moses and Elijah, but others say the real reason is because of the miracles they perform. It was Elijah who stopped the rain for three and a half years, so one of them must be him, and it was Moses who brought plagues upon the Egyptians, and turned the water into blood, so it must be him, too. But is God limited by who He works through? Can He not choose whom He will?

- The most likely candidates according to others are the apostles, Peter and Paul.

For us the safest interpretation is not to try to identify these two people at all (and they are people and not organisations or societies), but to accept that God will raise up two prophets to do His work at the right time. (Zechariah 4:1-3)

Verse 5: This verse implies there will be those who will seek to injure or abuse them; that is, that they would be liable to persecution. The fire that is spoken of here may or may not be real fire. The meaning of this image is possibly that they would have the power to destroy their enemies by their words, which would be as burning coals or flames of fire that would proceed out of their mouth. *'Anyone'*, it says, that desired to harm them would be destroyed in the same way. If this verse is to be taken literally, it presents a fearful reality, implying that God would cause fire to come down and destroy their enemies. But why not? It has happened before! (Numbers 16:35)

Verse 6: These men, and they are men, are not reincarnations or spiritual beings, have the power to control the weather, preventing rain from falling, they can turn water into blood and they can send any plague upon the earth whenever and wherever they wish. Despite attempts by some to spiritualise these miracles, there is no reason to do so and it is best if they are taken literally. What we can say is that if two men appear in the 'last days' performing miracles in the spirit and power of Moses and Elijah, then the terms of this prophecy will have been met. (1 Kings 17:1)

Verse 7: The word *'finish'* in this verse clearly shows that the period of their testimony will come to a determined end. Their end is brought about by the appearance of the *'beast'*, who rises from the bottomless pit and who battles against them, overcoming them and killing them. Just how these men are killed is not explained. The beast here is doubtless the Antichrist, the *'little horn'* mentioned in Daniel, chapter 8, manifesting himself here in all his diabolical power and justifying the title as the 'Man of Sin', as in 2 Thessalonians 2, verse 3.

Verse 8: Rather gruesomely it seems the witnesses' dead bodies are left lying in the street where they have fallen. The manner of their deaths is not made clear and the Greek version of this verse spreads a little confusion but, for us, the best solution is to accept the words as they are written. The question over what is *'the great city'* is debated extensively, some saying it must be Babylon or Rome, but it also appears to have spiritual connections with Sodom and Egypt. However, the last phrase of this verse surely confirms that the great city must be Jerusalem. (Jeremiah 23:14)

Verse 9: The meaning behind the words of this verse surely tells us that the wicked men of this world are so delighted at the deaths of these two, because of the nature of the testimony, that they refuse to permit burial. The *'three-and-a-half days'* is analogous of the three and a half years of the Tribulation period and in no way is it connected to the three days of Yeshua's time in the tomb. There are two possibilities to explain the words *'from the peoples, tribes, tongues, and nations will see their dead bodies'*. Firstly, as some suggest, there may be representatives of all these nations present in Jerusalem at that time but, secondly, and far more likely, the world's media would have been monitoring the scenes, would have captured all the events on camera, and every detail would be instantly transmitted around the world. (Psalm 79:2-3)

Verse 10: The early theologians had never heard of television, nor imagined such a system was possible, and it is this unawareness that lies behind their theory that the location of the events we are now looking at could not have been Jerusalem but was much more likely to have been Rome, with its Pope and worldwide influence. But through the technology available today, such an event as the death of two tormenting prophets would be known worldwide in moments. That's how the world will be able to rejoice and have parties and send presents.

Verse 11: But the rejoicing will be short-lived, for after the three-and-a-half days are completed, the breath of God will enter into them, and life will return to them miraculously and immediately. All those who witness this event will be filled with fear – and why not? (Ezekiel 37:9-10)

Verse 12: This verse speaks of a loud voice coming from heaven. *'And they heard'*, that is the two prophets heard these words: *'Come up here.'* They will be summoned to heaven and will go up in a cloud – and the world's television viewers will see them go. But, for them, there is yet more to come because three things will happen as the result of their coming resurrection, as we shall see in the next verse. It is these resurrections that begin the process that will extend over the final three and a half years of the Tribulation period leading, during this dreadful time, to the total regeneration of the Jewish nation – the remnant that survive!

Verse 13: In this verse we learn of three things that must happen almost immediately:

1. There will be a great earthquake that will destroy one tenth of the city, Jerusalem, and this should be taken literally...

2. ... and 7,000 people (Jews) will be killed, causing great fear among those who remain in the city and who will then give God the glory.

3. It is from this point on that the Jewish people will begin to turn towards God.

You should remember how Yeshua, when asked for a sign, said to the unbelieving Jews, in Matthew 12:39, that the only sign they would get would be the sign of Jonah, and that sign was given to them on three occasions:

1. Through the Messianic miracle of the resurrection of Lazarus, which they failed to recognise...

2. ... through the resurrection of Yeshua, which they rejected...

3. ... but now, through the resurrection of the two witnesses, they at last begin to take notice and to accept this as a sign of God's power.

Verse 14: The events of the second woe are now complete and those of the third woe are about to begin.

Verse 15: But before we go into detail, this verse tells us that the seventh angel will blow his trumpet and this will be followed by loud rejoicing in heaven. But why? What is there to rejoice about? It's all because a transfer of power has taken place. The kingdoms of this world have given way to the kingdom of God and His Messiah, who will reign forever, and to the saints who will reign with Him. (Daniel 7:27)

Verse 16 & 17: Then the twenty-four elders who were seated around the throne will fall on their faces in awe and admiration and worship God, giving thanks. They will probably be thinking less about being sharers of the great power and glory of God, but more because through His taking up that great power He will be answering the prayers of the saints and bringing His vengeance and justice.

Verse 18: The nations, controlled and manipulated by the Antichrist, will be furious at what is happening, but now will be the time for God's wrath to be poured out and very soon the judgement of all believers and the prophets will be executed and rewards given. At this time all the enemies who have sought to destroy the saints, Jews and Gentiles alike, will themselves be destroyed. (Psalm 2:1-3)

Verse 19: The temple of God in the heavenlies will be opened and the ark of the Lord's covenant, the holy of holies and the symbol of God's faithfulness to His own covenant people, will be seen in full. This is all accompanied with thunder and lightning, all the signs that the final outworking of heaven's judgement has come upon the Antichrist's world.

CHAPTER 12

Now it's time to move on, for here in this chapter we have verses specifically relating to the mid-Tribulation period and to the persecution of the Jewish people. For John this is yet another phase in his vision where he describes things that are past, are passing, or are prophetic.

THE MID-TRIBULATION PERIOD:

The woman, the child and the dragon – verses 1 to 6

¹Now a great sign appeared in heaven: a woman clothed with the sun, with the moon under her feet, and on her head a garland of twelve stars. ²Then being with child, she cried out in labour and in pain to give birth. ³And another sign appeared in heaven: behold, a great, fiery red dragon having seven heads and ten horns, and seven diadems on his heads. ⁴His tail drew a third of the stars of heaven and threw them to the earth. And the dragon stood before the woman who was ready to give birth, to devour her Child as soon as it was born. ⁵She bore a male Child who was to rule all nations with a rod of iron. And her Child was caught up to God and His throne. ⁶Then the woman fled into the wilderness, where she has a place prepared by God, that they should feed her there one thousand two hundred and sixty days.

Verse 1: In this verse and those following we have a concise summary of the First Coming of Yeshua and then of the activities of Satan. Here we read of a great sign that appears in the heavens, a sign of huge significance as well as great in scale. John saw a woman, clothed with the sun, moon and twelve stars. Who was she? And what did she represent? We can find out by turning to Genesis 37:9–11, where we have the story of Joseph, being then young and naive, unwisely relating a dream to his brothers where it is obvious that, in the dream, the sun represents Jacob, the moon is Rachel and eleven of the stars signify his brothers where he himself is the twelfth. This woman is not, as some say, the church, in any form at all, nor is she the Virgin Mary, nor is she any of the other fanciful theories that exist. Quite simply, the woman depicted here is representing the nation of Israel.

Verse 2: In this verse we read that she was heavily pregnant and experiencing the pains of childbirth. What does that mean? In the light of what follows, the child this woman (Israel) was bearing can be none other than Yeshua, the Messiah of Israel. Satan, following his first rejection back in the Garden in Eden (Genesis 3:14–15), had known the Messiah was coming. Nobody knew when that event might be, but when the Holy Spirit visited Mary the secret was out and Satan knew. (Micah 4:9-10)

Verse 3: It's here that we have Satan's reaction, for another sign appeared in heaven, this time a great, fiery red dragon with ten horns, and on its head seven diadems or crowns. There are many opinions as to what, or who, this dragon represents. That it is very large tells us of its great power, while the redness speaks of destruction and also corruption. Some say it is a picture of Imperial Rome, but others, because of what then follows, see that this is speaking of Satan himself. (Isaiah 27:1)

Verse 4: The symbolism of this verse has created many theories; one was that it was all fulfilled in the ecclesiastical world by Maximim, who ruled in the Asian element of the Roman Empire in 313AD. But that doesn't fit in with the context of this verse in any way. That this is speaking of Satan is certain, who, by devious means, has converted one third of the angelic host to his perverted way of thinking, and he now releases them to do his work in the world of humanity. The dragon (Satan) stood before the woman, symbolising in this way his hatred of the 'seed of woman', Yeshua, as was soon to be manifested through Herod's treachery and the cruel massacre of the innocent babes. (Daniel 8:10)

Verse 5: The woman gave birth to a male child, one that would come to rule the whole world with total authority, with a rod of iron. These words, cited from Psalm 2:9, leave us in no doubt as to who this child represents. And the child was caught up to heaven and to the throne of God, a sign of what was to come through the scene at Calvary. Without question this is Yeshua, and the vision John was seeing is referring to His historical birth. This is contrary to some who see this event as the crowning of Constantine as emperor of Rome, or others who see the child as the modern church and that this is speaking of the Rapture, all of which verge on fantasy. What is really foreshadowed here is the First Coming and then, in the following verses, we have a picture of the events leading to the Second Coming. (Isaiah 66:7)

Verse 6: This verse is speaking of the remnant of Israel (the Messianic believers) who flee to a place of security determined by God. It does not tell us here what the woman was fleeing from, but almost certainly it was from the advancing Antichrist's army that will gather at Armageddon prior to moving south towards Jerusalem. She, as representing the Jewish remnant, is doing what Yeshua had said to do in the passage in Matthew 24:16. A more detailed explanation of this verse will come later with verses 13 to 15.

War in heaven – verses 7 to 17

⁷And war broke out in heaven: Michael and his angels fought with the dragon; and the dragon and his angels fought, ⁸but they did not prevail, nor was a place found for them in heaven any longer. ⁹So the great dragon was cast out, that serpent of old, called the Devil and Satan, who deceives the whole world; he was cast to the earth, and his angels were cast out with him. ¹⁰Then I heard a loud voice saying in heaven, 'Now salvation, and strength, and the kingdom of our God, and the power of His Christ have come, for the accuser of our brethren, who accused them before our God day and night, has been cast down ¹¹And they overcame him by the blood of the Lamb and by the word of their testimony, and they did not love their lives to the death. [12] Therefore rejoice, O heavens, and you who dwell in them! Woe to the inhabitants of the earth and the sea! For the devil has come down to you, having great wrath, because he knows that he has a short time.' [13] Now when the dragon saw that he had been cast to the earth, he persecuted the woman who gave birth to the male Child. [14] But the woman was given two wings of a great eagle, that she might fly into the wilderness to her place, where she is nourished for a time and times and half a time, from the presence of the serpent. [15] So the serpent spewed water out of his mouth like a flood after the woman, that he might cause her to be carried away by the flood. [16] But the earth helped the woman, and the earth opened its mouth and swallowed up the flood which the dragon had spewed out of his mouth. [17] And the dragon was enraged with the woman, and he went to make war with the rest of her offspring, who keep the commandments of God and have the testimony of Jesus Christ.

Verse 7: In this verse we hear of another event, and it looks very bad for mankind. There is war in heaven, and Satan and all his demonic forces will be defeated by the heavenly host, God's army, under the command of Michael, the guardian angel of Israel and leader of the holy angels in their battles against evil. This war is also partly responsible for the woman's flight to a place of security provided for her. The question raised by this event is when this war is to happen. There are those who believe it happened at the time of the Messiah's ascension into heaven after His resurrection, while others see it as the casting out of paganism from the courts of the Roman Empire. There seems to be little agreement between the experts, but the most logical explanation is that this war will occur some time after the Rapture when Satan will still be accusing believers day and night before God. He will be rebuked by Yeshua who will send Michael, leading the armies of heaven against him. (Daniel 10:13)

Verse 8: In this war, Satan and his forces will be defeated and will find themselves outside the family circle of God, and there will now be no place found for him in heaven. (Job 2:1)

Verse 9: Now we learn that Satan, the great dragon, will be cast out of heaven and all his evil angels will be cast out with him. That is very good for heaven, since it says later that there will be much rejoicing there. But it will not be so good down here, though, for Satan will enter into the earth's environment where he will be confined throughout the second half of the Tribulation but, thankfully, it will only be for a short time. In the time that he has left he will wreak havoc, however. We find there are three words in this verse that define Satan's nature and reveal what mankind can expect from him. They are:

'Serpent': Cited from Genesis 3, verse 1, the deceiver.

'Devil': This is the Greek word for 'accuser' and 'slanderer'.

'Satan': The Hebrew word for 'adversary'.

Verse 10: John then heard a loud, or great, voice coming from heaven. Whose voice it is we are not told, but the general consensus is that it was the elders because of the term *'our brethren'* as it appears here. *'Now'* in this verse indicates that the time has at last been realised, and the words spoken are an introduction to the things that are about to occur. The casting out of Satan and all his angels is a sign that the dispensation of the kingdom of God, and the Second Coming, is soon to begin. This 'kingdom' is the Millennial Kingdom that will last for 1,000 years, the time of the Messiah's rule, ending when He delivers the kingdom to His Father, God, and the Eternal Kingdom will begin.

Verse 11: The voice continues and in this verse refers to the 'overcomers' who can be identified as the *'brethren'* of the previous verse. And *'they overcame him'*, that is Satan, as the consequence of the Lamb having shed His blood, without which none would be able to withstand Satan's accusations. *'The word of their testimony'* may mean that they faithfully testify to what the blood has done for them, even to death, which is right, but it may also mean more than words; that they overcame by the evidence of their lives.

Verse 12: Here we have the call to rejoice over all that has just been happening, but that call is addressed to the heavens and those that dwell in them. This must be speaking of angelic beings and the saints in Paradise, for there won't be much rejoicing on earth now that Satan is there. He feels cheated, he hasn't been able to halt God's plan of redemption, and he must take out his anger somewhere, or on someone;

that will primarily be on the Jewish people, but the whole world is going to suffer too. Satan will realise that he has only three and a half years left, for he has a clearer understanding of prophecy than we have, so, as his worst fears are about to be realised, he will set out on his programme for the systematic destruction of the Jewish people. Why the Jews specifically? It's because he knows that the Second Coming of Yeshua is totally dependent upon the Jewish people requesting Him to come.

Verse 13: In John's account, now that he has lost his place in heaven and had been cast down to earth, Satan decides to persecute the 'woman', Israel, from whom came the Messiah. In this verse we have the explanation for the deaths of millions of Jewish people, through the Crusades, the Inquisition, the Holocaust, and other atrocities. It is the result of the persecution, initiated by Satan, which is intended to destroy the Jewish people before they have opportunity to issue their invitation. This is the reason why Satan expresses his hatred of Yeshua, by taking it out on Yeshua's 'seed'. That the 'woman', as proposed by some, is the church being persecuted by the Jews following Yeshua's ascension is anti-Semitic rubbish and is not worthy of consideration.

Verse 14: Israel, therefore, is on the run, or at least the surviving remnant is, fleeing to a place of refuge in the desert prepared as a secure sanctuary by God. Yeshua, in Matthew 24:16, said *'flee to the mountains'*, while this verse from Revelation says *'wilderness'*, to a place already prepared for her, and she will be cared for (that means the remnant of Israel) for 1,260 days, the three and a half years of the second half of the Tribulation period. Note in this verse the implication that the people do flee successfully, or at least a proportion of them do, to a place reserved for them, and that place is believed to be Bozrah, also known as Petra, in what was Edom. The woman was given *'eagles' wings'*, which we can derive from Exodus 19:4 and Deuteronomy 32:11 to mean nothing more than successful flight to a place of refuge. The American Air Force is not involved, an idea based on the symbolism of the eagles' wings, nor will it be in evidence here, despite what one or two overexcited commentators have said. (Daniel 7:25)

Verse 15: In Satan's desperate efforts to prevent Israel's flight to safety, John saw him as spewing water out of his mouth. But is this really speaking about water? As we can imagine, the expectations of some theologians have been very creative. One sees the water as merely a figure of speech, another that it represents the nations of the world. Another view is that it portrays the flight of the believers to Pella from the armies of Rome in 70AD, which did happen, while a further view is that the enemy is the Saracens! And there are many others. But again, this event is entirely symbolic and surely the whole scene is depicting the waves of hatred and violent anti-Semitism that Satan is stirring up right now, and which is destined to get worse. (Hosea 5:10)

Verse 16: Some take this verse literally, but how can this be? It seems that the more sensible view is to take this symbolically too, and to see it as the help given to the believing Jews of the remnant in their isolation at Petra. Surely, as God sustained the Jews fleeing Egypt, as in Exodus, chapter 16, He can do the same here.

Verse 17: By this time the dragon, Satan, having missed his opportunity, is beside himself in a frenzy of rage and so he now goes *'to make war with the rest of her offspring'*. Who are we speaking of here? This question has produced many answers. Bearing in mind that these events take place after the Rapture, the most probable answer is that we are speaking of those who become believers of the gospel after that event, and those who are known as the Tribulation saints. We are, therefore, speaking of the fruit of the 144,000 Jewish evangelists. (Genesis 3:15)

CHAPTER 13

In turning to this chapter we shall see how John expands on the details of the Antichrist's period of activity, just as Daniel, in chapter 7 of his book, expanded on what he had said in chapter 2. John tells us that he saw a beast rising up out of the sea. Once again the sea represents the Gentile world and, as in Daniel, chapter 7, John is seeing the fourth beast.

The beast from the sea – verses 1 to 10

¹Then I stood on the sand of the sea. And I saw a beast rising up out of the sea, having seven heads and ten horns, and on his horns ten crowns, and on his heads a blasphemous name. ²Now the beast which I saw was like a leopard, his feet were like the feet of a bear, and his mouth like the mouth of a lion. The dragon gave him his power, his throne, and great authority. ³And I saw one of his heads as if it had been mortally wounded, and his deadly wound was healed. And all the world marvelled and followed the beast. ⁴So they worshipped the dragon who gave authority to the beast; and they worshipped the beast, saying, 'Who is like the beast? Who is able to make war with him?' ⁵And he was given a mouth speaking great things and blasphemies, and he was given authority to continue for forty-two months. ⁶Then he opened his mouth in blasphemy against God, to blaspheme His name, His tabernacle, and those who dwell in heaven. ⁷It was granted to him to make war with the saints and to overcome them. And authority was given him over every tribe, tongue, and nation. ⁸All who dwell on the earth will worship him, whose names have not been written in the Book of Life of the Lamb slain from the foundation of the world. ⁹If anyone has an ear, let him hear. ¹⁰He who leads into captivity shall go into captivity; he who kills with the sword must be killed with the sword. Here is the patience and the faith of the saints.

Verse 1: At this time, John found himself standing on the seashore, but we are not told which sea it was, possibly the Mediterranean, or maybe just a visionary one. He tells us that he saw the fourth beast, the one seen by Daniel, rising up out of the sea, which symbolises the confused and disordered nations of the world. It had ten horns, each having a crown upon it, but then we are told it had seven heads. This is new, and for explanation we must wait until we get to chapter 17. We learn that each of the seven heads bears a blasphemous name. It is not clear from any source what this actually means, nor is it clear that it is the same name on each head, or seven different ones, but as the names are blasphemous it would seem likely that they ascribe to the heads some qualities or characteristics that rightly belong to God alone but have been corrupted. (Daniel 7:3)

Verse 2: This verse explains in a nutshell the nature and character of the beast spoken of in Daniel 7:7. We can see that this fourth beast, or kingdom, has elements of all three of the great empires of the past, the lion-like mouth of Babylon, the bear-like feet of the Medo-Persian, and the leopard-like body of the Greek. And we shall also see here that the dragon, that is Satan, transfers all civil power and authority to the beast, using him as an instrument of his hatred, thus John is clearly speaking of the Antichrist stage or period of control. As one commentator says, the beast is used by the dragon as the instrument of every form of evil. (Daniel 7:4-6)

Verse 3: In this verse we are told that one of the seven heads appeared to have been mortally wounded, but the wound that caused the death was healed. This is a perplexing passage in a chapter that is already a difficult one to interpret, and there are many opinions about it. The suggestion that the beast seen here is speaking of Papal Rome can surely be dismissed. That it represents the Roman Empire is possible, at least worthy of consideration, having lost power in the fifth century but revived and functioning in Europe today. The best thing one can say about almost all of the opinions that have been given is that there is much confusion. One proposal that seems to be accepted by many is that there will be a counterfeit resurrection, that the seventh head is the Antichrist who, for whatever reason, will have been killed but who will be publicly raised from the dead by Satan. Such is part of the deception, for there is no reason to believe that Satan has the power to raise anyone from the dead, and if the Antichrist is the seventh head, what do the other six represent?

Verse 4: It is through this act of gross deception that the world will turn to worship the dragon, who is Satan, leading on to the worship of the beast, the Antichrist, who is elevated to the position properly held by Yeshua. So much of this is the consequence of modern civilisation where progress in thought, science, education and art has led people into apostasy and blasphemy. Although the beast has been given power, he uses it for his own purposes, as determined by his master, Satan. The question *'Who is like the beast?'* has an echo in Exodus 15:11, *'Who is like unto thee…?'* (KJV) And the phrase *'Who is able to make war with him?'* implies a desire on Satan's part to bring war and destruction to those who will not worship the beast. (Daniel 8:24)

Verse 5: The beast is given a mouth, by that meaning that it is God alone who, in fulfilment of His purposes, permits the beast to use his mouth as he does. The words that are spoken are words of great arrogance and self-glorification, and the beast is allowed to continue his evil work during the forty-two months, the three and a half years, of Daniel's 'seventieth week'.

Verse 6: This verse, together with verse 7, expands on verse 5, saying how the beast uses his mouth to slander God Himself, especially fulfilled through the wrongful use of the names on his heads. He also defames God's tabernacle, meaning heaven, and denigrates the angelic host and the souls of departed saints.

Verse 7: Again we see there is nothing the beast can do that is not sanctioned by God. *'It was granted to him'* reminds us that it is God who has brought this period of tribulation upon all those on the earth at this time. The Antichrist is permitted to exercise control over the whole earth to establish his empire, with a few exceptions, as we shall see, all in fulfilment of God's purposes. However, in this verse there is an implied question: Who are the 'saints'? On the basis of what we have already understood, the saints are the remnant of both the Jewish and the Gentile believers just prior to the return of the Messiah. We may also see the prophetic words of Yeshua, in Matthew 24:9–12, being fulfilled at this time:

> ⁹*Then they will deliver you up to tribulation and kill you, and you will be hated by all nations for My name's sake. ¹⁰And then many will be offended, will betray one another, and will hate one another. ¹¹Then many false prophets will rise up and deceive many. ¹²And because lawlessness will abound, the love of many will grow cold.*

Verse 8: Here we are told that every person on earth, all those whose names are not written in the Lamb's Book of Life, will worship the beast. These are the unbelievers, those who sign up to the Antichrist's cause but who will subsequently perish. The meaning of this is that there will be those dwelling on the earth at that time whose names are written, with many others, in the Lamb's Book of Life, and must be considered as those who come to believe following the Rapture. All that is happening here is pointing to the great and final apostasy prophesied by our Lord in Matthew 25:11–12 and of which we may read in 2 Thessalonians 2:3–4:

> ³*Let no one deceive you by any means; for that Day will not come unless the falling away comes first, and the man of sin is revealed, the son of perdition, ⁴who opposes and exalts himself above all that is called God or that is worshipped, so that he sits as God in the temple of God, showing himself that he is God.*

Verse 9: This verse suggests that all these events, as they occur, will be understood only by those with the ability to discern the times. (Ezekiel 1:24)

Verse 10: Greek scholars have problems with their understanding of this verse, because of the lack of clarity in the text, but there is a warning contained within it which confirms that, no matter what those referred to actually do, they are still operating within God's control, and judgement is surely coming upon them. Here, also, God gives comfort to the saints of the Tribulation period, those who will be saved after the Rapture but, as the result of the ministry of the 144,000, will be swept into the kingdom. They are to experience some of the harshest treatment of any period of history, but God is saying here that whatever is done to them will be done to their persecutors, only more so, and God is advocating that they have patience for He will surely avenge His elect, Jews and Gentiles together. (Jeremiah 15:2)

The advent of the False Prophet – verses 11 to 15

¹¹Then I saw another beast coming up out of the earth, and he had two horns like a lamb and spoke like a dragon. ¹²And he exercises all the authority of the first beast in his presence, and causes the earth and those who dwell in it to worship the first beast, whose deadly wound was healed. ¹³He performs great signs, so that he even makes fire come down from heaven on the earth in the sight of men. ¹⁴And he deceives those who dwell on the earth by those signs which he was granted to do in the sight of the beast, telling those who dwell on the earth to make an image to the beast who was wounded by the sword and lived. ¹⁵He was granted power to give breath to the image of the beast, that the image of the beast should both speak and cause as many as would not worship the image of the beast to be killed.

Verse 11: It is now that we read of another event that will occur in the mid-Tribulation period, and that is the appearance of another beast, this time the False Prophet. Yeshua warned about false prophets, in Matthew 7 and Matthew 24, and many have come and gone, and many more are still here, but this one is a bit special. In this verse he is described as *'another beast'* and from these words, and through the things he does, we can see him as the counterfeit of the Holy Spirit. There seems to be no significance in the number of horns other than they express the resemblance of a lamb, and are probably identifying false prophetism. (Daniel 8:3)

Verse 12: In this verse we learn that this person, and he will be a person, has all the authority of the Antichrist and, just as the Holy Spirit has authority from Yeshua, so the False Prophet will use his authority to cause the people to worship the Antichrist. We are reminded here of the first beast's *'deadly wound'* that has been healed, spoken of in verse 3, and it is this miracle that explains the people's willingness to adore him. Who administered that wound we are not told.

Verse 13: This is another of those verses that generate much speculation. Would the signs John saw, as performed by the False Prophet, whoever he proves to be, be real or merely figments of John's imagination? Those who promote the belief that this beast which he saw was Papal Rome would say that they were not real, just imagination. Others say the miracles were real and were performed through demonic power. Some say that bringing down fire from heaven is speaking of a false Pentecost. The truth is that we cannot be sure, but it is more logical to believe that these deceiving signs will be real, when they happen, rather than that in some strange way they refer to Rome or are merely imagination. (1 Kings 18:38)

Verse 14: We see here that the False Prophet was able to demonstrate the power, given him by Satan, through many false miracles, but note that everything is subject to the will of God. By working miracles the False Prophet is able, through deception, to lead the world into idolatry and the worship of the Antichrist. We know that, even today, we are being bombarded by 'signs and wonders' ministries, most of which are as counterfeit as that of the False Prophet, and we should understand that signs and wonders, in themselves, prove nothing. Many are the people being led astray by things that may have the appearance of being good, but have their roots in evil. There is a mistaken belief that because it seems good it is good, and therefore must be of God. Most often it is not God at all, but nonetheless that doesn't impact on countless biblically naive people, and so many are moving into seductive temptation with their eyes wide open but with their spiritual perception totally blanked off.

However, we learn here that the beast appears to have received a death wound from a sword. In today's parlance that may mean an assassination attempt using a machete or perhaps a gun. The False Prophet then instructed those who dwelt on the earth to create on image to *'the beast who was wounded by the sword and lived'*. What sort of image and who is this speaking of? There is little doubt that in

100

the time of the Antichrist's reign, stress will be laid on the fact that although he had received a fatal wound, nevertheless he had lived. Thus it will be that just as Yeshua's authority to reign was through His death and resurrection, so the Antichrist's resurrection will establish his right to claim divine authority and to demand worship. The image, therefore, appears to be of the Antichrist, but just what that means is not made clear. It's a little bit speculative, but could this image be the 'Abomination of Desolation' spoken of by Daniel (Daniel 12:11) and warned about by Yeshua in Matthew 24:15–16 and Mark 13:14? If so, this is the time for the Jewish believers to flee to the place of security – Bozrah.

Verse 15: Now we find the False Prophet is able to give life to an inanimate object, this created image of the beast, whatever it is, by so doing convincing more people to worship it. Isn't it interesting that men are now able to clone living beings? Is this what John is telling us will happen here? Could it be that the False Prophet, whoever he is, will be able to create a clone of the Antichrist? Just recently, too, it has been reported that scientists have created life out of something that was not alive. Primitive life, yes, but it may well be the beginning of something bigger and truly sinister. Be that as it may, there is no indication as to just who or what this image resembles, but for those who will not worship it, the penalty will be death. There is, as you can imagine, such variety in the interpretations of this passage, and it is questionable whether we can get to a true understanding. Some say it may be that this is speaking less of an image of a person but more of a corrupt form of authority, political or religious, but that doesn't fit the description here.

The mark of the beast – verses 16 to 18

16He causes all, both small and great, rich and poor, free and slave, to receive a mark on their right hand or on their foreheads, 17and that no one may buy or sell except one who has the mark or the name of the beast, or the number of his name. 18Here is wisdom. Let him who has understanding calculate the number of the beast, for it is the number of a man: His number is six hundred and sixty-six.

Verse 16: The False Prophet will now demand that every individual in the world, rich and poor, should carry the mark of the beast. Just as the true believer has the mark of the Holy Spirit, a seal that is visible only to God, invisible to all others, although other believers are able to identify its presence, a seal that is a guarantee of salvation, so the False Prophet produces a counterfeit seal. Just as masters have branded their slaves in the past, so here we have a question. Will this mark be a brand, or will it be a rubber stamp? What we do know is that this mark is said to be '*on their right hand or on their foreheads*', the most conspicuous parts of the body. Some suggest that the mark is self-applied by those who have readily submitted to the Antichrist, but there is no evidence to confirm this supposition.

Verse 17: This seal, or mark, is the guarantee for making a living and for buying and selling, and there has been much speculation as to its form. Some suggest a chip inserted under the skin. Others suggest a tattoo, while still more think it will be an identity card of some kind. There are two other stipulations associated with the mark, for each must bear the name of the beast or the number of his name in some form. But whatever it is, there is an unidentified mark that identifies the followers of the Antichrist. It is the mark that will be placed upon those who recognise Satan as being God and worship him, and it is the mark by which he recognises those who do believe in him. As an aside consider the move to a cashless society where every purchase is made by debit or credit card. Just think about the possible implications with such a system.

Verse 18: The whole issue in this verse is a mystery, a fact confirmed by the words '*Here is wisdom*', and real spiritual discernment is required. The meaning of the number is revealed in this verse, and we shall see that five clues are given:

1. It is the name of the beast.
2. It is the number of his name.
3. It is the number of the beast.
4. It is the number of a man.
5. The number is 666.

So, on the one hand, we see that the Antichrist uses the number 666 as his special mark which must be worn by all who accept him, but at the same time we can see that the number gives us a clue as to who he is, because the number is the number of his name and, according to Hebrew tradition, it will be a name that has the numerical value 666. Each letter of the Hebrew alphabet has a numerical value. In English, for example, we could give each letter of our alphabet a number, A=1, B=2, etc., and so it is with Hebrew. The first nine letters are numbered 1 to 9, the next nine are numbered in tens up to ninety, the remainder in hundreds up to 400, making up the twenty-two letters of the Hebrew alphabet. There may be a complication because the English Bibles are translated from the Greek, therefore we should be able to understand that we cannot calculate a name in advance, but that as the Antichrist appears we can confirm it is him by the numerical value of his name. Incidentally, it is not the Pope, nor is it any of the least popular politicians we could mention. Just one brief addition to this, for six is the number of incompleteness, and therefore 666 is incompleteness repeated three times, never making perfection. There are other suggestions that some say points to Rome, but the truth is that until the Antichrist is revealed this mystery will not be resolved.

Chapter 14

Having given much time to the events of the previous chapter, we shall now move on to study chapter 14. It is in this chapter that we find there are seven mid-Tribulation proclamations made that have three purposes:

1. To predict the total failure of the satanic programme and the exposure of the counterfeit trinity.

2. To announce the effects of the seven bowl judgements during the second half of the Tribulation period, and

3. To give encouragement to those who will stand fast because, although the first half of the Tribulation has been harsh, it is going to be much worse from now on.

The Lamb and the 144,000 on Mount Zion – verses 1 to 5

¹Then I looked, and behold, a Lamb standing on Mount Zion, and with Him one hundred and forty-four thousand, having His Father's name written on their foreheads. ²And I heard a voice from heaven, like the voice of many waters, and like the voice of loud thunder. And I heard the sound of harpists playing their harps. ³They sang as it were a new song before the throne, before the four living creatures, and the elders; and no one could learn that song except the hundred and forty-four thousand who were redeemed from the earth. ⁴These are the ones who were not defiled with women, for they are virgins. These are the ones who follow the Lamb wherever He goes. These were redeemed from among men, being firstfruits to God and to the Lamb. ⁵And in their mouth was found no deceit, for they are without fault before the throne of God.

Verse 1: This verse marks a sharp contrast with the previous vision, beginning as it does with the words: *'I looked, and behold'*, which suggest a much more dynamic beginning to what is to follow. This vision is intended to give the believers here on earth a pledge to encourage them to stand fast in adversity, for they will attain to the same glory described here. Some say the 144,000 must be in heaven and that the Mount Zion here spoken of is the heavenly Mount Zion, others that this is a scene on earth. Surely this latter suggestion is the correct one, for there is no reference in scripture to a Mount Zion being anywhere but in Jerusalem. It is now that we are given details of what was sealed on the foreheads of these evangelists – the name of God. (Psalm 2:6)

Verse 2: John heard a voice from heaven, effectively bringing the first of the seven proclamations which were to open up for him the vista of the Millennial Kingdom. He saw what it is going to be like after the Tribulation period ended – the four living creatures, the twenty-four elders, the glorious singing, and the praise. Why is it, thinking about it, that this scene is introduced at this particular point, when we are dealing with the Tribulation period? The purpose, quite simply, is to show that all Satan's efforts will come to nothing; his programme of destruction will not succeed. What is the evidence for that assurance? Well, to start with we see the 144,000 have been kept safe and secure. These are the ones with God's mark on their foreheads – not so those who bear the mark of Satan, for they are doomed to destruction and the *'second death'*. The voice John hears is most likely coming from angels in heaven, and the sounds of the harps, those in the hands of the twenty-four elders, all accompanied by the 144,000 on earth as we read Revelation 15:8. (Ezekiel 1:7)

Verse 3: Now we read about the song these redeemed ones sing, a song that only they know because it is special for them, written, no doubt, by Yeshua Himself, who is of the tribe of Judah, and Judah means praise.

It's a new song, referring to the faithfulness of God and of Yeshua, where all believers, Jews and Gentiles alike, will be redeemed from all the trials and persecutions of the Antichrist's period of rule. (Psalm 144:9)

Verses 4 & 5: In these two verses we read of the character of the 144,000:

1.   They have never married, choosing to remain celibate.

2.   They follow Yeshua wherever He goes.

3.   They are the first fruits of a harvest that is just beginning. For there to be a first logically implies there will be others. As we have said, they will not be the only ones saved during this time, but they are the first.

4.   They are without a lie. They are pure within, and without defilement by the world, by self or by Satan.

5.   They are without blemish, being pure on the outside too, in attitude and behaviour.

More proclamations of the angels – verses 6 to 13

⁶Then I saw another angel flying in the midst of heaven, having the everlasting gospel to preach to those who dwell on the earth – to every nation, tribe, tongue, and people – ⁷saying with a loud voice, 'Fear God and give glory to Him, for the hour of His judgment has come; and worship Him who made heaven and earth, the sea and springs of water.' ⁸And another angel followed, saying, 'Babylon is fallen, is fallen, that great city, because she has made all nations drink of the wine of the wrath of her fornication.' ⁹Then a third angel followed them, saying with a loud voice, 'If anyone worships the beast and his image, and receives his mark on his forehead or on his hand, ¹⁰he himself shall also drink of the wine of the wrath of God, which is poured out full strength into the cup of His indignation. He shall be tormented with fire and brimstone in the presence of the holy angels and in the presence of the Lamb. ¹¹And the smoke of their torment ascends forever and ever; and they have no rest day or night, who worship the beast and his image, and whoever receives the mark of his name.' [12] Here is the patience of the saints; here are those who keep the commandments of God and the faith of Jesus. [13] Then I heard a voice from heaven saying to me, 'Write: "Blessed are the dead who die in the Lord from now on."' 'Yes,' says the Spirit, 'that they may rest from their labours, and their works follow them.'

Verse 6: Now we have the appearance of another angel, the first of six and in addition to those we've already met, having the message of the true gospel, the good news that Yeshua died on the cross for the sins of the world, and bringing the second proclamation. The concept that this is a message only for the Gentiles is not credible. This message is the final call to the whole world and every person living.

Verse 7: The call is for all people everywhere to turn from wickedness and the ways of the Antichrist's world and to respond to the Creator, to the gospel of truth. We see that it follows the call of the Antichrist, in chapter 13, for the world to worship him, and for those who have accepted the mark it is now too late to change. But for those who have not so committed themselves the call goes out to all humanity – who will you worship, the true God or the false? The urgency is for an immediate decision, for the hour of judgement has come. And the call will be in a language all will be able to understand, and it will say, 'Choose now, who is God!' (Nehemiah 9:6)

Verse 8: Then, in this verse, we have the third proclamation delivered by the second angel. This time it contains the prediction of the fall of political Babylon, the Antichrist's headquarters, and of all things opposed to God. This Babylon is the symbol of secular power, arrogance and cruelty, but it is not Rome as some argue. Ecclesiastical Babylon has already gone, all religious activity stopped, but now the time has come for Satan's stronghold to be destroyed. All this will happen during the period when the war, known as the Armageddon Campaign, is nearing its conclusion, but more about that when we come to study the eight stages of that campaign. The Babylon here is that evil city, built on the banks of the Euphrates River, broken but not eliminated in the past, and to be rebuilt as the political capital of the Antichrist. And this city has already been partially rebuilt, in a fashion, as part of the legacy of

Saddam Hussein, who probably never realised he was being used by Satan to fulfil his strategy. It has been, and probably still is, the centre of magic, wizardry and satanic worship. (Isaiah 21:9)

Verse 9: The fourth proclamation is found in this and the next two verses, brought by the third angel. The point made here is that those who have gone so far as to accept the mark of the beast and see the Antichrist as some sort of god, now have no way back. However, with the angel's words *'If anyone worships the beast...'* the condition implied leads us to the conviction that there will be those who do not, and will not worship the beast, and for them God's mercy will remain available.

Verse 10: Those who have submitted to the will of the Antichrist will soon discover there is nothing left but the wrath of God, and that will be very unpleasant. They will taste the wine of God's wrath in which there will be no trace of grace, hope or compassion. Right up until this moment there has still been an opportunity to escape judgement, through repentance, but once the decision has been made to worship the Antichrist, that is one step too far. The punishment reserved up until now for the Antichrist will be the experience of those who have fallen into the trap, for they will be tormented with brimstone and fire. (Isaiah 51:17)

Verse 11: This verse is clearly speaking of the final destination of all sinners, those who have worshipped the beast and his image, together with the Antichrist and the False Prophet, and that is eternity in the Lake of Fire. Paul, in 2 Thessalonians 2:3–5, and again in verses 8 to 12, predicts the falling away into satanic worship. It is in verse 8 of Paul's letter that we read of the *'brightness of His coming'*, which is speaking of Yeshua's Second Coming in glory, and leading to the total destruction of Satan's power. (Isaiah 66:24)

Verse 12: We may see in this verse that the certainty of eternal punishment and everlasting torment for the wicked is the basis of, and encouragement for, the patience and endurance of the saints.

Verse 13: The fifth proclamation comes in this verse in the form of a special blessing for the martyrs of this period. Undoubtedly, all martyrs who lose their lives for Yeshua are blessed, including all those from the first half of the Tribulation, but in this verse we see that for those *'dead who die in the Lord'* there will, from that time on, be a special blessing, presumably because they will have had to withstand the worst of the atrocities. That these are Tribulation saints is fairly clear but, having suffered much worse cruelty than those earlier, are deserving of a special blessing. The blessings, therefore, come especially from their being freed from the awful suffering they have endured during the recent times, and they will be rewarded in the glory that is to come. There they will be able to rest from their troubles, all the persecution they have experienced, and their record will go before them. This is guaranteed because it is the Holy Spirit who ratifies it.

The Messiah's coming, and the prelude to Armageddon – verses 14 to 20

14 Then I looked, and behold, a white cloud, and on the cloud sat One like the Son of Man, having on His head a golden crown, and in His hand a sharp sickle. 15 And another angel came out of the temple, crying with a loud voice to Him who sat on the cloud, 'Thrust in Your sickle and reap, for the time has come for You to reap, for the harvest of the earth is ripe.' 16 So He who sat on the cloud thrust in His sickle on the earth, and the earth was reaped. 17 Then another angel came out of the temple which is in heaven, he also having a sharp sickle. 18 And another angel came out from the altar, who had power over fire, and he cried with a loud cry to him who had the sharp sickle, saying, 'Thrust in your sharp sickle and gather the clusters of the vine of the earth, for her grapes are fully ripe.' 19 So the angel thrust his sickle into the earth and gathered the vine of the earth, and threw it into the great winepress of the wrath of God. 20 And the winepress was trampled outside the city, and blood came out of the winepress, up to the horses' bridles, for one thousand six hundred furlongs.

Verse 14: In this verse we have the sixth proclamation where John, in his vision, saw a white cloud, a prelude to the clouds of glory of the Second Coming, and seated on the cloud he saw Yeshua Himself, wearing the crown of victorious triumph, and wielding in his hand a sharp sickle. In this instance the sickle is the symbol of the beginning of judgement and of the harvest of sinners, for the time of judgement has come. We may therefore understand from this that despite all the activities of the Antichrist, and the persecution directed at believers, there will be vengeance. (Daniel 7:13)

Verse 15: Another angel now appeared, *'out of the temple'*, sent out from God with a message for His Son, Yeshua, in the form of a command: *'Thrust in Your sickle and reap'*. Why? It's because at last judgement has come, the time all creation has been waiting for, groaning, and reminding us the words of Yeshua, in Mark 4:29:

> *But when the grain ripens, immediately he puts in the sickle, because the harvest has come.*

Verse 16: So, Yeshua, seated on the cloud, swings with His sickle and the earth is reaped. We may understand from this, then, that because of all the activities of the Antichrist, and the persecution directed at the Jewish people and all believers, there is yet to be a great harvest for judgement.

Verse 17: Now the fourth angel emerged from the heavenly temple, he too having a sharp sickle. We are coming now to the seventh and final proclamation, in which this new angel will also come with a sickle in his hand, and this time it is for another purpose. The sickle being used here is a symbol of the completeness of the judgement about to come, where the harvest gathered is destined for total destruction. We have here the fulfilment of the prophetic words spoken of by Yeshua in Matthew 13:30:

> *Let both grow together until the harvest, and at the time of harvest I will say to the reapers, 'First gather together the tares and bind them in bundles to burn them, but gather the wheat into my barn.'*

Verse 18: Yet another angel then appeared, but note that this angel, making his proclamation in a loud voice, is not the angel with the sickle but is one who comes out from the altar and has power over fire, probably the fire on the altar. The altar is the one we read about in Revelation 6:9; in 8:3 and in 16:7, and is the altar beneath which are the souls of the martyrs, crying out for vengeance. The command given to the angel with the sickle will be to thrust it in and with it to gather the clusters on the vine of the earth, for the grapes are ripe. (Joel 3:13)

Verse 19: The angel with the sickle gathers the clusters of grapes and throws them into the winepress of God's wrath. The reality of the image of a winepress and the bursting and crushing of the grapes is being used here to define the effects of God's wrath on those who have rejected Him. That the vine is symbolic of Israel says much, but this is not necessarily excluding Gentiles, who will also be judged. (Isaiah 63:1-6)

Verse 20: The nature of God's judgement is expressed in this verse as being incredibly severe upon the enemies of Yeshua at the time of the destruction of the Antichrist. The final clash of the Armageddon Campaign is being portrayed here; the final destruction of the armies of the Antichrist outside the city, Jerusalem, and a defeat where men's blood rises as high as a horse's bridle over a distance of 1,600 furlongs. What does this measure signify? Is it literally a distance of about 200 miles? Or is it, as some argue, a symbolic figure derived from the square of four, the number that means the world, multiplied by the square of ten, the sign of completeness, and thus indicating that no one, anywhere, can escape the judgement of God? It could be both. Other suggestions are:

a. That it is forty (the symbol of punishment) multiplied by forty so as to suggest the most terrible and complete punishment.

b. That it defines the Kidron Valley leading to the Dead Sea that will be filled with blood.

c. A more likely possibility is that it is the distance from Jerusalem to Bozrah, and we shall explore this in more detail later.

There are other ideas, too, some quite elaborate and fanciful, but the best answer is the simplest, that it merely denotes that the slaughter will be great, and that we cannot tell for sure why the figure of 1,600 has been given. Therefore, the meaning doesn't matter very much and it's best left as it is written.

CHAPTER 15

We have now reached the point where we shall consider the several stages of the second half of the Tribulation period beginning, in this chapter and the next, with the events heralding the return of the Messiah. The seventh seal judgement led us to the trumpet judgements, and the seventh trumpet judgement leads us into the time of the bowl judgements. We are now at the stage described in Revelation 11:14–15, for the second woe is past, but the third woe, even more severe, is about to come, for it contains the seven bowl judgements. The seventh trumpet will be sounded and then the greatest woe and terror ever known will fall upon the inhabitants of the earth. The woes God has permitted Satan to exact upon the Jewish people have been especially hard, but now it is the time of God's woe, when His wrath has fully come, with a total reckoning upon the evil that exists, but also with final deliverance for all His chosen few. We must note confirmation of this from the second half of verse 15, which says, *'The kingdoms of this world have become the kingdoms of our Lord and of His Christ'.*

As we think about the bowl judgements we shall see that this is exactly what they are, and that all the bowl judgements are contained within the seventh trumpet judgement. They are released simultaneously upon the world through the blowing of that trumpet. In some translations the word 'kingdoms' is not in the plural but is singular, and this is the more correct since it has been Satan's kingdom, the one-world Antichrist kingdom that has now fallen to the Messiah. The total and final fulfilment of this judgement will not be complete until the end of the three and a half years, but the end is surely coming.

The purpose of the second half of the Tribulation is made clear by the twenty-four elders in Revelation 11:16 to 18, which is that those who have been destroying the earth will themselves be destroyed. The achievement of this destruction will be through the seven bowl judgements, and verse 19 of Revelation 11 describes the scene in heaven, the temple being opened up and with a view of the Ark of the Covenant. The lightning, voices, thunderings, an earthquake and great hail are presumably experienced on earth, although that detail is missing. The ark found in this verse is located in heaven, and is not the one modelled upon it and was once installed in the temple. That disappeared at the time of Nebuchadnezzar.

This chapter is the prelude to the release of the seven bowl judgements upon the earth.

The second half of the Tribulation period – verses 1 to 8

[1]Then I saw another sign in heaven, great and marvellous: seven angels having the seven last plagues, for in them the wrath of God is complete. [2]And I saw something like a sea of glass mingled with fire, and those who have the victory over the beast, over his image and over his mark and over the number of his name, standing on the sea of glass, having harps of God. [3]They sing the song of Moses, the servant of God, and the song of the Lamb, saying: 'Great and marvellous are Your works, Lord God Almighty! Just and true are Your ways, O King of the saints! [4]Who shall not fear You, O Lord, and glorify Your name? For You alone are holy. For all nations shall come and worship before You, for Your judgements have been manifested.' [5]After these things I looked, and behold, the temple of the tabernacle of the testimony in heaven was opened. [6]And out of the temple came the seven angels having the seven plagues, clothed in pure bright linen, and having their chests girded with golden bands. [7]Then one of the four living creatures gave to the seven angels seven golden bowls full of the wrath of God who lives

forever and ever. ⁸The temple was filled with smoke from the glory of
God and from His power, and no one was able to enter the temple till
the seven plagues of the seven angels were completed.

Verse 1: In this verse, as John looked, he saw seven angels who simultaneously appeared, each having the wrath of God in the form of different plagues, where these will be the last of the judgements, signifying the nearness of the end and the victorious return of the Messiah. Just how they have them is not clear, for it is not until verse 7 that they are given their bowls. Great and marvellous is their appearance, not only because of the way they look, but also because of the terrible events that are associated with them. (Leviticus 26:21)

Verse 2: John then saw what he describes as a sea of glass, but just what that is and who the people are that stand on it is not made clear. It has been speculated upon by many, as can be imagined. It would seem reasonable, despite all the debates and guesswork, to see these people as Tribulation saints, those who have come to faith in Yeshua through the Tribulation period and have paid the ultimate price for it. The sea of glass mingled with fire would accord with the majority view that in this case the sea represents the fullness of God's joy while the fire symbolises judgement. However, there is nothing to clarify this meaning, so it is left to one's personal and individual interpretation. The harps serve only for the praise of God.

Verse 3: Having said all that, however, this verse gives credence to the thought of martyred saints who have overcome and conquered through spiritual warfare. They are those who have not submitted to the Antichrist nor have taken his mark, and thus they sing the song of Moses. Which song is not quite clear, whether it is the one recorded in Exodus 15:1–18, or the one in Deuteronomy 32:1–43. Who but the Jewish remnant would sing the song of Moses? But they also sing the song of the Lamb, and the words of that song are recorded here and in the following verse. Surely this verse is speaking about the remnant of both Jew and Gentile believers. (Psalm 92:5; Psalm 139:14)

Verse 4: The song continues in this verse so that the nations referred to here must be the same as those in verse 3, all the people of the world who were unbelievers but have resisted the Antichrist's onslaught and survived during this time, and who will be converted through Yeshua's return. The overriding cause for this will be that God's judgements will have prepared all hearts to receive His mercy. There is some debate about whether the Lord, coming in clouds of glory, will gather up these elect before or after destroying the enemy.

Verse 5: It is then that John saw the temple of the tabernacle in heaven had been opened, just how is not clear. The temple here is not referring to the 'Holy of Holies' but to the 'Holy Place'. It is called the 'temple' because it is the special place of testimony to the presence of God among His people. (Exodus 38:21)

Verse 6: From out of the temple *'the seven angels'* appear, the definite article meaning these are the ones we've met before, seemingly with the seven plagues, but just what that means is unclear. In John's vision they are wearing bright linen clothing, the symbol of purity, and around their chests are golden bands, or girdles, the sign of righteousness. (Exodus 28:6)

Verse 7: One of the *seraphim* then gave to each of the seven angels a golden bowl filled with God's wrath. Just what is in the bowls that represents God's wrath is not clear, but some argue that it would have been a noxious and poisonous liquid. We don't know, so it is unwise to guess. (Jeremiah 25:15)

Verse 8: And the temple was filled with the smoke of the glory of God, the *Shekinah*, and which would remain there until the plagues and their effects were complete. The several views as to what the smoke represents are too obscure to be worth mentioning here. (2 Chronicles 5:13-14; Isaiah 6:1-4)

Chapter 16

The seven bowls, in some Bible versions they are called vials, referred to in this chapter are vessels containing the wrath of God, which manifests itself in the form of fearful sicknesses and diseases that will bring great suffering, even death, to men and women upon the earth, on those who bear the mark of the beast. God is now beginning, in a direct way, to bring an end to the period known as the Great Tribulation, through which the faithful have been passing, and will bring His judgement against the Antichrist and all his followers. So, for the next little while let us examine the consequences attached to the pouring out of each bowl, or vial.

The seven bowl judgements – verses 1 to 11

¹ Then I heard a loud voice from the temple saying to the seven angels, 'Go and pour out the bowls of the wrath of God on the earth.' ² So the first went and poured out his bowl upon the earth, and a foul and loathsome sore came upon the men who had the mark of the beast and those who worshiped his image. ³ Then the second angel poured out his bowl on the sea, and it became blood as of a dead man; and every living creature in the sea died. ⁴ Then the third angel poured out his bowl on the rivers and springs of water, and they became blood. ⁵ And I heard the angel of the waters saying: 'You are righteous, O Lord, the One who is and who was and who is to be, because You have judged these things. ⁶ For they have shed the blood of saints and prophets, and You have given them blood to drink. for it is their just due.' [7] *And I heard another from the altar saying, 'Even so, Lord God Almighty, true and righteous are Your judgments.'* [8] *Then the fourth angel poured out his bowl on the sun, and power was given to him to scorch men with fire.* [9] *And men were scorched with great heat, and they blasphemed the name of God who has power over these plagues; and they did not repent and give Him glory.* [10] *Then the fifth angel poured out his bowl on the throne of the beast, and his kingdom became full of darkness; and they gnawed their tongues because of the pain.* [11] *They blasphemed the God of heaven because of their pains and their sores, and did not repent of their deeds.*

Verse 1: We read now that John heard a loud voice, this time it is believed to be the voice of God, that came out of the temple and from the midst of the *Shekinah*, saying *'Go and pour out the bowls'*. These bowls contained the wrath of God that would bring great suffering, even death, to men and women upon the earth who bore the mark of the beast. That they were not poured out in heaven must be fairly obvious, and it is acceptable to believe that the angels will temporarily leave their heavenly abode and move into the space between heaven and earth. (Jeremiah 10:25)

Verse 2: The first bowl was poured out upon the earth. The result was that foul and loathsome sores appeared on men and women alike, implying that this is a skin condition that may well be cancerous, a possible explanation if this verse is taken literally. There are those who suggest that this should be viewed from an allegorical perspective – in other words, this verse reveals a tremendous outbreak of social and moral corruption, of atheism, vice and utter depravity. But this interpretation is hard to accept since we are talking here of God's judgement which will be directed against such things, and the lawlessness that has already come in through the *'man of lawlessness'*. Far rather the literal interpretation is the most acceptable one. The sores appear only on those who have accepted the mark of the beast, so the contents of the bowl obviously don't affect everyone – the remnant spoken of in the previous chapter will not be affected. Could it be that the mark, implant or otherwise, will react in some way because of this judgement? (Exodus 9:9-11)

Verse 3: The second bowl was then poured out upon the earth. Here we have the account of the completion of the operation that began with the second trumpet judgement. With this bowl the remaining two thirds of the sea will be polluted, turned into blood, dead men's blood according to John's view, thick and lifeless, and everything in the sea will die. If this is the true understanding, a very serious food shortage will begin at the time this happens because fish, and the fruit of the sea, will cease to exist. However, there are those who see the sea in this instance representing the restless state of the nations of the earth. We shall only know the true interpretation as the events portrayed are worked out in the future.

Verse 4: Then the third bowl was poured out upon the earth. The effect of the pouring out by the third angel is described in this and the next two verses. Just as with the waters of the sea, all fresh water, water for drinking, will now be turned into blood, for the reason explained in verse 6. (Psalm 78:44)

Verse 5: Then the *'angel of the waters'* spoke. This was not the third angel who had just emptied his bowl but is the one appointed by God to be responsible for the streams and rivers. Note here the familiar words *'was and who is to be'* that do not include the words *'is to come'* and that is because, at the time when all this happens, the Lord will be in the process of coming. Note, too, that *'judged these things'* is in the past tense – by the time all this happens the judgement will have been completed, it's the sentence that is now being carried out. (Psalm 145:17)

Verse 6: A great shortage of drinking water will begin at this point as the judgement that began in Revelation 8:10 is completed and all fresh water will become blood. The judgement is that those who directly, or indirectly, shed the blood of the martyrs should have only blood to drink. In other words they deserve what they get. There are those who question that the water is actually turned into blood, for of course this is all pictorial language, but there is no reason for taking this verse as anything but literal. What John is seeing, therefore, is the polluting of all the waters by being changed into blood. (Isaiah 49:26)

Verse 7: John heard another voice, apparently from the altar. Is this another angel standing near the altar – or is the altar personified so that the altar itself is able to speak? The altar speaks, just as the blood of Abel is said to speak (Luke 11:51), and how the stones of Jerusalem (Luke 19:40) are said to cry out. As in many other instances, the various explanations for this verse are incoherent and are not worthy of serious examination. It has nothing to do with the French Revolution as Elliott of the Historical School proposes. As with so much of this book the simplest answer is often the best. (Psalm 19:9)

Verse 8: The fourth bowl was then poured out, but this time it is upon the sun. In this verse and the next we read of the outcome, which is that the heat of the sun will increase to such an intensity as to scorch men and women as though with fire.

Verse 9: And yet, despite all this, the people blame God, blaspheming against His name and failing to repent. The content here suggests that the mercy of God may still be available to those who turn to Him, even at this very late hour, among those who have not accepted the 'mark'. Already we have warnings of depleted ozone layers and the dangers associated with sunburn, therefore we can see how things are already moving in that direction, but this will be much, much worse than anything so far experienced. Note the parallel with the fourth trumpet judgement where the natural light sources were affected.

Verse 10: Now the fifth bowl was poured out upon the earth. In this verse and the next we have the effects of this outpouring by the fifth angel. This judgement will strike directly at Babylon, the political headquarters of the beast, the seat and source of the stability of the authority given him by Satan. This brings the fourth blackout as the Antichrist's kingdom becomes full of darkness, and everywhere will be confusion and pain, so intense that men will gnaw their tongues with anguish. (Exodus 10:21-23)

Verse 11: And still there appears to be a way out, through repentance, but men reject it and blaspheme against God because of their pains and sores, too blind to accept that release is still possible. What this verse reveals is that the first three plagues continue to be effective and that all are cumulative and do not succeed each other.

Preparation for the Armageddon Campaign – verses 12 to 21

¹²Then the sixth angel poured out his bowl on the great river Euphrates, and its water was dried up, so that the way of the kings from the east might be prepared. ¹³And I saw three unclean spirits like frogs coming out of the mouth of the dragon, out of the mouth of the beast, and out of the mouth of the false prophet. ¹⁴For they are spirits of demons, performing signs, which go out to the kings of the earth and of the whole world, to gather them to the battle of that great day of God Almighty. ¹⁵'Behold, I am coming as a thief. Blessed is he who watches, and keeps his garments, lest he walk naked and they see his shame.' ¹⁶And they gathered them together to the place called in Hebrew, Armageddon. ¹⁷Then the seventh angel poured out his bowl into the air, and a loud voice came out of the temple of heaven, from the throne, saying, 'It is finished!' ¹⁸And there were noises and thunderings and lightnings; and there was a great earthquake, such a mighty and great earthquake as had not occurred since men were on the earth. ¹⁹Now the great city was divided into three parts, and the cities of the nations fell. And great Babylon was remembered before God, to give her the cup of the wine of the fierceness of His wrath. ²⁰Then every island fled away, and the mountains were not found. ²¹And great hail from heaven fell upon men, each hailstone about the weight of a talent. Men blasphemed God because of the plague of the hail, since that plague was exceedingly great.'

Verse 12: The sixth bowl was then poured out upon the earth. It is here, in this verse, that we see the effect this sixth bowl judgement has upon the great river Euphrates. The purpose for doing this is that the river will be dried up to make possible the way for *'the kings from the east'* to invade the land areas north of Israel. What is meant by the *'kings from the east'*? Ignoring the wild speculations of some, that they were Parthian invaders allied to Nero, the general consensus is that the real understanding of the words is that the *'kings'* represent the forces and leaders of the seven nations allied to the Antichrist. With the Antichrist's headquarters being in Babylon, it is this fact that identifies the *'east'* and it will be from here that the *'kings'* will march, with their forces, to gather at *Har-Magedon* (Armageddon) to do battle against Israel, and against God and the Lamb. Biblically the 'east' means the area known as Mesopotamia which lies between the two rivers, Tigris and Euphrates, in the middle of which lies Babylon, due east from Israel and about 500 miles distant. The assertion that the Euphrates in this verse is not a river but is the Ottoman army of Turkey, as existing in 1820, does not deserve further comment. (Jeremiah 51:36)

Verse 13: In this, and the next three verses, John introduces a different theme. He saw three unclean spirits having the appearance of frogs. The sources of these spirits are the mouths of the three main villains in this account, the dragon (Satan), the beast (the Antichrist) and the False Prophet. This sounds revolting, and it is, for the symbolism here appears to explain these spirits as being uncleanness, offensiveness and pollution of the most disgusting kind. (Exodus 8:6)

Verse 14: This verse tells us that this is the work of the counterfeit trinity, sending out very powerful spirits where their purpose is to reinforce the evil spirits that are already at work in the nations and that have allied themselves with the Antichrist. The intention is to remove any resistance there might be among the nations to fighting in this war. Just what these three frogs represent is the source of much debate – seeing they come from the mouth of the dragon – and the best interpretation is that, together, they represent every evil power imaginable, total depravity. The battle that is about to commence, known incorrectly as the Battle of Armageddon, is aimed first of all at Israel, but the final battle is for the kingship of the world. It is a battle that will end with the glorious appearing of the Lord Yeshua, coming in clouds of glory, and the shattering defeat of the enemy. (1 Kings 22:21-23)

Verse 15: This verse is an exhortation from the Lord to be ready, and watching for his coming. The picture portrayed here is of a watchman, the true believer, ready clothed and fully armed, on the lookout for a 'thief'. His garments symbolise righteousness, worn because of faith in Yeshua and without which he would be ashamed, and where shame, in this context, is speaking of humiliating defeat through unpreparedness. That the 'thief' in this instance is Yeshua, the One who is coming, is clear from this verse – there is no doubt about it. According to Paul, in 1 Thessalonians 5:2, His coming will be at night, but this does not necessarily mean in darkness, it is far more probable that this is meaning that His appearance will occur when the darkness of sin will be at its worst.

Verse 16: The words *'And they gathered'* is confirming the role of the three frog-like evil spirits, who will gather the armies of *'the kings from the east'* at the place called Armageddon. In Hebrew the name *Har-Magedon* means 'Hill of Magedon', while *Ar-Magedon* means 'City of Slaughter', the place where the Canaanite kings were overthrown in the days of Barak and Deborah, which casts some doubt on the normal understanding of the name. It seems that the name *Har-Magedon* is more correctly given to an area rather than to a specific place such as a city, and correctly defines a battleground. It is generally believed that this is found at the western end of the Valley of Jezreel. This valley lies between the hills of Galilee, to the north, and the mountains of Samaria to the south. In the valley is a river that flows east into the Jordan while, at the opposite, western end of the valley, is the city of Megiddo, hence its name. It is this valley that is believed to be the place at which the armies of the Antichrist will be gathering, but that no battle takes place there. (Zechariah 12:11)

Verse 17: The seventh bowl was then poured out. Here the angel appeared to scatter the contents of his bowl into the air, at which time a loud voice spoke the words, *'it is done'*, which means that whatever event is the subject here, it has been done and completed. The first time these words were recorded they were spoken by Yeshua from the cross, for He had completed, through His sacrifice, God's plan for the redemption of all mankind. At that time, the price of redemption had been paid, but now, in this new situation, we have the completion of all God's plans with the judgement of all mankind.

Verse 18: Then loud noises were heard, possibly the sounds of war, with thunder and lightning, and a mighty earthquake, the desolation from which must have been colossal. Whether or not this is the great earthquake which will divide the Mount of Olives it doesn't say, but it may well be, or one of a series as the whole world is being changed. This verse does not describe the effects of the seventh bowl judgement, only the beginning of them.

Verse 19: There is much debate over this verse as to which city is the *'great city'*. Some say Rome, but that is unlikely. Others say it must be Babylon, because of the sin it represents. Others say it must be Jerusalem, which will become the seat of the Antichrist and a place of unbelief. But many of the cities of the world will be destroyed at this time, so which is correct? As Babylon is referred to in this verse this seems to be the most probable *'great city'*, being divided into three parts, where the meaning is that the city will be broken up and overthrown, sustaining severe damage during this war. However, because of the words of chapter 11, verse 13, it could be Jerusalem, but equally the cities of Babylon and Jerusalem may be considered as synonymous and both may be the subject here. The suggestions that the *'great city'* is Papal Rome, or some other heathen city, should not be considered seriously. Although it doesn't say so, this destruction will almost certainly include the third temple, which will have been completed not long before. It is at this time that political Babylon, the evil capital of the Antichrist, will be obliterated as the result of God's wrath. Many other cities will be broken down during this time because judgement will be universal, but Babylon will fall because an army of the righteous will rise up to destroy it, and Israel will then be restored. This is confirmed through the words of Jeremiah, in Jeremiah 50:1-5.

Verse 20: It seems that John is aware of islands and mountains disappearing, even though, at this time, the world remained intact. Some commentators see the islands and mountains as symbolising nations and kingdoms, and that may be correct. Taking this verse literally may also be correct, because earthquakes and natural convulsions could easily produce this effect.

Verse 21: Adding to all the other geographical disasters, it tells us in this verse of hailstones, big ones, not the little pea-sized stones we may be used to, but great blocks of ice, weighing, according to the text, about thirty kilograms each. But still the people moan and groan and blaspheme, at least those who have not been killed by the hailstones do. Not surprising, really, but there is still a way out for some. The destruction of Babylon is given more prominence in the next few chapters. (Exodus 9:18-19)

CHAPTER 17

THE JUDGEMENT OF BABYLON

This chapter is still referring to events of the first half of the Tribulation period. In it we shall deal with the period of rule of ecclesiastical Babylon, the false and apostate church. This term describes the religious system that will be in place at this time, and we shall see what that means as we study these verses. Twice already we have had the introduction to the fall of Babylon, in chapters 14 and 16, but in this chapter and the next there is a detailed account of it. Finally, the events recorded here refer to the time immediately prior to the Second Coming.

Who is the 'great harlot'? – verses 1 to 7

¹Then one of the seven angels who had the seven bowls came and talked with me, saying to me, 'Come, I will show you the judgment of the great harlot who sits on many waters, ²with whom the kings of the earth committed fornication, and the inhabitants of the earth were made drunk with the wine of her fornication.' ³So he carried me away in the Spirit into the wilderness. And I saw a woman sitting on a scarlet beast which was full of names of blasphemy, having seven heads and ten horns. ⁴The woman was arrayed in purple and scarlet, and adorned with gold and precious stones and pearls, having in her hand a golden cup full of abominations and the filthiness of her fornication. ⁵And on her forehead a name was written: MYSTERY, BABYLON THE GREAT, THE MOTHER OF HARLOTS

AND OF THE ABOMINATIONS OF THE EARTH. ⁶I saw the woman, drunk with the blood of the saints and with the blood of the martyrs of Jesus. And when I saw her, I marvelled with great amazement. ⁷But the angel said to me, 'Why did you marvel? I will tell you the mystery of the woman and of the beast that carries her, which has the seven heads and the ten horns.'

Verse 1: In this verse we have an angel, one of the seven who had brought the seven bowl judgements, probably the seventh, approaching John and inviting him to follow and to see the vision of the judgement of the great harlot. Harlotry, or prostitution as it is widely known, is the taking of something that is normal, proper and good and converting it into something that is abnormal, improper and potentially evil. A prostitute uses sex, and that is how we find it described in Hosea 1 and 2, and elsewhere. In the context here we are not talking about sexual activity, but spiritual prostitution and harlotry, and God's judgement of it. The harlot spoken of here is not a woman, although the image suggests it, but is representative of a new religious order. So it is that this 'woman' rules over all the religious affairs of the world, the coming one-world religion being propagated by the current Pope and others. The fact that she sits on many waters tells us that her influence is felt worldwide. Can we identify her? The most likely view among many is that she represents the apostate, one-world church that is being formed even now, comprising Catholicism in its every form, plus unrepentant Protestantism, false sects and religions, even paganism and witchcraft. (Nahum 3:4-5)

Verse 2: The spiritual fornication as described here was being committed, in John's vision, by the kings of the world, signifying nations and governments, and all the people of every strata of society who had sold out to the Antichrist. The methods used by this harlot are those of seduction that draw men away from the worship of the true God, tempting them with worldliness, wealth and influence, into the worship of the beast. The drunkenness described here is not that caused by alcohol, but is that which clouds the mind into believing lies and deception. (Isaiah 23:17)

Verse 3: John was then taken on a spiritual journey to a place somewhere in the wilderness. There we learn that he saw the harlot seated upon a scarlet-coloured beast, a beast covered with blasphemous names, having seven heads and ten horns, as already seen in chapter 13. This reveals to us that this beast is the Antichrist, who has control of all the nations, who will ensure that the harlot has the full support of kings, rulers and governments in her ecclesiastical ambitions for unquestioned authority. In other words the 'woman', represented on earth by the one-world state church, will dominate and manipulate the nations to fulfil her lifelong desire for total worldwide religious supremacy. (Daniel 7:7)

Verse 4: The woman can be seen to be immensely wealthy, for she is dressed in clothes of purple and scarlet and is wearing ornaments of precious stones and gold. There are many Protestant theologians who see the colours of purple and scarlet in the robes of the cardinals of Papal Rome, and this suggestion is reasonable if we relate this to the comments in verse 1 of this chapter. She holds in her hand a golden cup or chalice which is full to the brim with the abominations and filthiness of her harlotry. Some argue that the cup contains the blood of the martyred saints, referred to in verse 6, but this is not an acceptable theory and it is probably more correct to say that the contents of the cup are used to corrupt the nations to commit uncleanness and spiritual debauchery. (Jeremiah 51:7)

Verse 5: In this verse we learn the name of the harlot, written on her forehead, the customary place for a symbol, or frontlet, that advertises a harlot's profession. Very briefly let us consider and dissect this name:

- 'Mystery': There are those who view this word as a unique part of the name, but the more convincing argument is that it is defining the mystical character of what immediately follows it.

- 'Babylon the great': In this description, Babylon may be seen as the spiritual representation of the whole of the Antichrist's empire.

- 'Mother of harlots': She is the chief of all harlots, the founder of all harlotry, and the mother of apostasy in the unrepentant church and the promoter of all spiritual immorality.

- 'Abominations of the earth': This phrase identifies the totality of her evil influence in all the world's administrations – secular and religious.

This 'woman' may reasonably be identified as the 'bride of the Antichrist', the counterfeit of the 'bride of the Messiah'.

Verse 6: John realises, as he observes this woman, that she is *"drunk with the blood of the saints and with the blood of the martyrs of Jesus".* This helps us to answer the question raised earlier when we were considering the judgement under the fifth seal and how it affected the Tribulation saints. The question we asked, *'How were they saved?'* can be answered as being through the ministry of the 144,000. The second question asked was *'Who killed them?',* and here is the answer – by the persecution by ecclesiastical Babylon, the worldwide counterfeit church made up of every false cult and religion. Remember the words of Yeshua to the disciples, in John 16:2 and 3, where He says:

> *'They will put you out of the synagogues; yes, the time is coming that whoever kills you will think that he offers God service. And these things they will do to you because they have not known the Father nor Me.'*

Verse 7: John is amazed at what he sees, and this will be the response of many who will find it hard to believe that the church could descend into murder, mayhem and every form of perversion. History, however, reveals that there are precedents when we look at the legacy of Papal Rome, through the Crusades, the Inquisition and every kind of fornication. This will be repeated, only more so, and it will be a worldwide Holocaust. The angel asked John why he should marvel at what he sees and then told him that the mystery of the 'woman' and the beast is about to be revealed. This is just as well, for there are some who see this 'woman' as the same one who appears in Revelation 12! That the 'great harlot' is Israel, considered to be so by some apparently godly and intelligent men, is a monstrous lie and reveals a desperate lack of biblical understanding.

The meaning of the 'Beast' and 'The Scarlet Woman' – verses 8 to 18

⁸The beast that you saw was, and is not, and will ascend out of the bottomless pit and go to perdition. And those who dwell on the earth will marvel, whose names are not written in the Book of Life from the foundation of the world, when they see the beast that was, and is not, and yet is. ⁹Here is the mind which has wisdom: The seven heads are seven mountains on which the woman sits. ¹⁰There are also seven kings. Five have fallen, one is, and the other has not yet come. And when he comes, he must continue a short time. ¹¹And the beast that was, and is not, is himself also the eighth, and is of the seven, and is going to perdition. ¹²The ten horns which you saw are ten kings who have received no kingdom as yet, but they receive authority for one hour as kings with the beast. ¹³These are of one mind, and they will give their power and authority to the beast. ¹⁴These will make war with the Lamb, and the Lamb will overcome them, for He is Lord of lords and King of kings; and those who are with Him are called, chosen, and faithful.' ¹⁵Then he said to me, 'The waters which you saw, where the harlot sits, are peoples, multitudes, nations, and tongues. ¹⁶And the ten horns which you saw on the beast, these will hate the harlot, make her desolate and naked, eat her flesh and burn her with fire. ¹⁷For God has put it into their hearts to fulfil His purpose, to be of one mind, and to give their kingdom to the beast, until the words of God are fulfilled. ¹⁸And the woman whom you saw is that great city which reigns over the kings of the earth.'

Verse 8: Now, in this and the following verses, John was going to be given an explanation as to what it all meant. The beast in this verse is the same as the beast of chapter 13, the Antichrist, and is also the same beast as found in Daniel, chapter 7. In order that we may understand something of what follows we must turn to this chapter in Daniel, and to the visions Daniel had, and the nations represented by them:

- The Babylonian Empire.

- The Medo-Persian Empire.

- The Greek Empire.

- The Roman Empire.

The first three kingdoms have disappeared into antiquity, apart from a few carvings and scattered stones, and so has the old Roman Empire, except that its legacy remains, even today, in the form of Imperialism. Let us first see what we may discover about the fourth kingdom, the Roman Empire, which has undergone several stages of development. These are identified, at the stage we are now, as we read Daniel 7:23–27:

- It starts as a united kingdom.

- It develops into a one-world government, as seen from the phrase '*... shall devour the whole earth*'.

- This is followed by the division into ten kingdoms.

- Finally, the Antichrist stage – i.e. the little horn.

Note the progression. The Antichrist is not scheduled to appear until the end of the ten-kingdom stage, but when he does appear he will destroy three of the ten. How this will happen we are not told, whether militarily or economically, but they will be overcome in some way. He will speak great things, against God and against the saints, and will change the times and the seasons. But his days are limited and after three and a half years, he and all he stands for will be destroyed by God. Then will come the fifth and final kingdom, the Millennial, or Messianic, kingdom that will last for 1,000 years and will be essentially Jewish.

The expression '*was, and is not*', by occurring twice in this verse is obviously speaking of the same beast, the one we have already met, the Antichrist. Once again we see here reference to the Antichrist appearing on the scene, apparently having been killed but, in reality, only wounded, descending into the '*bottomless pit*', and then being 'resurrected', but that at the end he will go into perdition, the eternal Lake of Fire. This verse confirms that it will be those whose names are not written in the Lamb's Book of Life who will be those that worship him as divine through witnessing his restoration. (Exodus 32:32-33)

Verse 9: The angel continues with his explanation to John with the words *Here is the mind which has wisdom*. He is saying here that spiritual discernment is necessary in order to understand the symbolism contained in these verses. The seven heads, he tells John, are seven mountains upon which the woman sits. Following biblical symbolism, the seven mountains represent seven kings or seven kingdoms; they do not mean Rome as some believe, even though it is built over seven hills.

Verse 10: This verse, continuing from verse 9, serves to clarify the meaning. It tells us that the seven hills are indeed kingdoms, because we now read of seven kings or, more correctly, kingdoms. We then learn that at the time John was looking, five kings had fallen and were no more, one was in existence at that time and one was still to come. The five kings that have fallen can reasonably be interpreted to mean Egypt, Assyria, Babylonia, Medo-Persia and Greece, the one that 'is' being the sixth, Rome, as in John's day. Bear in mind that today we are living in the age of Roman imperialism which has continued from Roman times until today. We are now in the time of the seventh kingdom, the Antichrist's kingdom, which will become utterly ruthless and autocratic during the Tribulation period but, when that time finally does come, it will only last a short while.

Verse 11: Here is a confusing verse. How do we understand this? The Antichrist is the eighth king and yet he is also one of the seven? In explanation, the one-world government stage will divide into ten separate kingdoms ruling concurrently and signified by the ten horns but, from Daniel 7:20, we learn that the Antichrist will destroy three of them. There are, therefore, seven kingdoms that remain and so, when the Antichrist takes up his rule, he will be the eighth. But then, from verse 10, we learned of seven kingdoms, represented by six periods of historic rule that have existed consecutively, soon to be followed by the seventh, the Antichrist, and he will rule for the second half of the Tribulation period, for three and a half years.

Verse 12: This verse confirms what we have just learned about the ten horns, that they are ten kingdoms but, at the time John was writing, they did not exist, and still they do not. Soon, however, they will receive their authority from the Antichrist, but it won't last for long. Note that the move for globalism through several secretive organisations has already divided the world into ten economic zones, so all is prepared. These kingdoms represent those nations of the world that ultimately will join forces to make war against God's people. They correspond to the ten toes of Nebuchadnezzar's image and the ten horns of Daniel's beast. They will receive their power from the Antichrist *'for one hour'*, for a very short period of time. (Daniel 7:24-25)

Verse 13: These ten kingdoms are all in total agreement; at least they are at the beginning, being of one mind and united in purpose, and they individually give away their rights to the Antichrist.

Verse 14: This appears to be speaking of the Armageddon Campaign, when the nations of the world will join together with the particular aim of destroying Israel. But the armies of these kings, under the control of the Antichrist, will be destroyed by Yeshua Himself at some later time, as we shall see. Implied here is the victorious return of the Messiah, in glory, accompanied by the saints, the chosen ones in heaven.

Verse 15: The angel then explained to John that the waters he had seen, in verse 1, on which the great harlot sat, are representative of the population of the whole world, every nation and language.

Verse 16: It's here that we find the harlot will be hated by the kings as well as by the Antichrist (and probably by the people), and she will be ravaged and destroyed by them when she is at the peak of her power. Why they should hate her is not clear at this moment, but this verse anticipates what is coming. Those who were formerly her 'lovers' will desert her and she will be stripped of all her wealth, which is colossal. To *'eat her flesh'* means that all her huge wealth and treasures will be taken from her, and she will be burned with fire, the legal punishment for harlotry. And so, the destruction of Mystery Babylon will be complete; the one-world religious system operating through the first half of the Tribulation period will be no more. (Leviticus 21:9).

Verse 17: Why will these nations turn so violently against her? It is because the Lord will decide when the time of her harlotry will be over and He will use the kings to accomplish His will. They thought all they were doing was according to their own will, but God had decided to end the reign of the harlot and they were the means by which her end would be achieved.

Verse 18: This verse confirms that the woman John has seen, the harlot, who has been identified as ecclesiastical Babylon, the one-world apostate church, is the same as the great city, Mystery Babylon. There are no distinctions between them. This is not so for political Babylon, the physical capital and administrative centre of the beast, the Antichrist. Looking back to the question of who the *'great harlot'* is, the suggestion that she exclusively represents Rome, in some form or another, can surely be discounted and we may recognise, from the conditions existing in much of the church today, that the logical conclusion is that she is representative of the whole apostate church emerging today including, and probably led by, Rome.

CHAPTER 18

Having seen the severe manner in which mystical Babylon is to be destroyed, we now examine the issues of physical, or political, Babylon's destruction. When will these prophecies of her destruction be accomplished? From John's perspective the destruction will be at some future date, although at the time he was writing there was very little of historic Babylon still standing. If Babylon is to be destroyed as predicted by the prophetic word and the city is not, as some say, just a spiritual symbol representing the centre of all immorality and corruption, or even Papal Rome according to some, then she must be reconstructed prior to the time of the end. This reconstruction has been taking place over some years now, but is very incomplete. From God's word we know that her prophesied destruction comes during 'The Day of the Lord', the Tribulation period, where one of the most significant passages describing that day can be found in Isaiah, chapter 13. Read it to understand more fully what God's judgement is all about.

A warning to leave Babylon – verses 1 to 8

¹After these things I saw another angel coming down from heaven, having great authority, and the earth was illuminated with his glory. ²And he cried mightily with a loud voice, saying, 'Babylon the great is fallen, is fallen, and has become a dwelling place of demons, a prison for every foul spirit, and a cage for every unclean and hated bird! ³For all the nations have drunk of the wine of the wrath of her fornication, the kings of the earth have committed fornication with her, and the merchants of the earth have become rich through the abundance of her luxury.' ⁴And I heard another voice from heaven saying, 'Come out of her, my people, lest you share in her sins, and lest you receive of her plagues. ⁵For her sins have reached to heaven, and God has remembered her iniquities. ⁶Render to her just as she rendered to you, and repay her double according to her works; in the cup which she has mixed, mix double for her. ⁷In the measure that she glorified herself and lived luxuriously, in the same measure give her torment and sorrow; for she says in her heart, "I sit as queen, and am no widow, and will not see sorrow." ⁸Therefore her plagues will come in one day – death and mourning and famine. And she will be utterly burned with fire, for strong is the Lord God who judges her.

Verse 1: John had a visit from another angel, obviously a very powerful one, which means it could be an archangel, although it does not say. That it says it was *'coming down from heaven'* clearly indicates it was another one, for the previous one was already down. This angel was clothed in glory to the extent that he will illuminate the whole earth with his brilliance. Despite his appearance, it was not the Messiah, nor the Holy Spirit, and definitely not Martin Luther, as suggested by one theologian! (Ezekiel 43:2)

Verse 2: This angel brought a proclamation against Babylon, crying with a loud voice that her destruction was near. He cried out with a loud voice so that his message would resound all around the world, to be heard by all, especially those who have subjected themselves to the authority of Babylon, and to strike the hearers with awe and fear. The Babylon spoken of here is political Babylon, not ecclesiastical Babylon, because that has already fallen through the destruction of the harlot, as we have just learned. Thus we find that political Babylon will come to an end as a city, both literally and as a symbol of the Antichrist's kingdom, and it will become a desolation, a habitation for all demons and demonic beings, to be confined in the remains during the 1,000 years of the Messiah's reign, but to be totally destroyed at the end. (Isaiah 34:13-15)

Verse 3: The angel's message continued with a condemnation of all the corruption and sin that Babylon held within itself and that it had come to represent. The reference here is not so much to material wealth but to spiritual things – idolatry, witchcraft and superstition, where the harlot, as the apostate church, had used men to her own ends, and men had used her for theirs. Through the corruption that existed, many men had made themselves wealthy beyond measure, through their pride and hypocrisy, but in doing so they had laid themselves open to the coming judgement which will sweep them and their wealth away. (Jeremiah 51:7-8)

Verse 4: Another voice is heard, not the voice of the church, as some argue, nor is it the voice of God or of His Messiah. We can be certain of that, because of the nature of the lament. Without doubt this was an angel speaking in the name of Yeshua. As earlier, a call was made for the Jewish people in the city to flee, for if they don't, they, too, will suffer the coming judgement. That this is speaking about Jews is clear from the expression *'my people',* where the only Gentiles will be those bearing the seal of the Antichrist. (Jeremiah 51:6)

Verse 5: Babylon's sins have been so great and so numerous that they have become heaped up so as to reach to heaven, but God will remember them all, and will repay them in kind. But before the destruction can begin, the Jews among the inhabitants must leave and, taking the message with them, they must head towards Jerusalem to report to the remnant still there the fact that, as they left, the destruction of Babylon had begun. (Jeremiah 51:9)

Verse 6: Just as the nations have done to the Jews, through persecution, violence and murder, so they are to be repaid in the same way, only double. This is God's indictment for all that has been done and, as it says, the contents of the cup that the corrupt city, Babylon, has filled with the poison of hatred and anti-Semitism, this will be multiplied to Babylon twice over. (Jeremiah 50:15)

Verse 7: Babylon, this city that boasted the counterfeit trinity, that had vaunted herself against the God of heaven, had lived a life of luxury. Personified here, she said she was enthroned as a queen because her husband was the world power of that time, and she would never experience sadness or loss. When the time comes political Babylon will lose everything. (Zephaniah 2:15)

Verse 8: Therefore, because of all the sin, boasting and pride that she has shown, it will be all change for this evil city, for all in one brief period of time, everything will be turned around and she will experience all what will follow:

- death, which will make her a widow;

- mourning, that which she said could never happen;

- famine, as her wealth and luxury will be removed from her;

- and she will be burned with fire which, in accordance with Old Testament law, is the just punishment for corruption. (Isaiah 47:9)

Reading on in this chapter, we have the lamentations of those who are going to lose out because of the destruction of Babylon. Those lamenting will fall into three distinct categories – firstly, the kings, by which we mean the leaders of the nations; secondly, the merchants, those who made their money out of trade and business, banking, etc.; and thirdly, the ship owners, those whose business it was to transport luxury goods for fat profit. Their lamentations are of a purely selfish nature – there is no love in any of these relationships, just the desire for power and wealth.

The world laments over Babylon – verses 9 to 19

⁹The kings of the earth who committed fornication and lived luxuriously with her will weep and lament for her, when they see the smoke of her burning, ¹⁰standing at a distance for fear of her torment, saying, 'Alas, alas, that great city Babylon, that mighty city! For in one hour your judgment has come.' ¹¹And the merchants of the earth will weep and mourn over her, for no one buys their merchandise anymore: ¹²merchandise of gold and silver, precious stones and pearls, fine linen and purple, silk and scarlet, every kind of citron wood, every kind of object of ivory, every kind of object of most precious wood, bronze, iron, and marble; ¹³and cinnamon and incense, fragrant oil and frankincense, wine and oil, fine flour and wheat, cattle and sheep, horses and chariots, and bodies and souls of men. ¹⁴The fruit that your soul longed for has gone from you, and all the things which are rich and splendid have gone from you, and you shall find them no more at all.

¹⁵The merchants of these things, who became rich by her, will stand at a distance for fear of her torment, weeping and wailing, ¹⁶and saying, 'Alas, alas, that great city that was clothed in fine linen, purple, and scarlet, and adorned with gold and precious stones and pearls! ¹⁷For in one hour such great riches came to nothing.' Every shipmaster, all who travel by ship, sailors, and as many as trade on the sea, stood at a distance ¹⁸and cried out when they saw the smoke of her burning, saying, 'What is like this great city?' ¹⁹They threw dust on their heads and cried out, weeping and wailing, and saying, 'Alas, alas, that great city, in which all who had ships on the sea became rich by her wealth! For in one hour she is made desolate.'

Verse 9: In this verse and the next we again read of the *'kings'*. Undoubtedly this is speaking of the seven kings and all the ministers and governors of those nations that have allied themselves to the Antichrist and have ruled under his authority. They were committed to this wanton city, political Babylon, and had benefited through its power, but at the cost of their own freedom and independence. (Jeremiah 50:46)

Verse 10: But now they will seek to withdraw from the city in an attempt to avoid the consequences of the judgement that is coming so swiftly upon her. Will it literally be all over in one hour? Probably not, because a 'day', in the biblical sense, can mean an undefined but possibly short period of time, and much the same probably applies to the term *'one hour'*. There are many theologians who see these descriptions in the figurative sense, that this is not speaking of a physical Babylon but some mystical destruction of the apostate church, or even Papal Rome, but there can be little justification from scripture for accepting such arguments in the full light of all the prophecies. These *'kings'*, the remnant of the ten, will be looking on what is happening from what they hope is a safe distance. Because the Antichrist has been gathering his army at Armageddon, they will certainly be there, but somehow will be aware of what is happening from miles away, as they stand in the Jezreel Valley. Television, social media and the internet perhaps? (Isaiah 13:1)

Verse 11: Here we find it is also time for the merchants to lament over what is happening. Their sadness is probably not so much because of the destruction of the city as the destruction of their trade empires. Because political Babylon will, at this time, be the commercial centre of the world, these people, probably women as well as men, will be the high-flyers of the business world, the executives, bankers, etc. The reason they weep and mourn is that the markets they have relied on will have totally dried up.

Verses 12 & 13: These verses itemise those commodities that would be considered as essential for such luxury living in this great city. Verse 13 ends with reference to the bodies and souls of men. This may mean literal slaves, forced labour, but it is equally possible that it means the souls of men enslaved to wealth and position.

Verse 14: It is not clear who is speaking these words that are interjected here and are addressed to political Babylon. Some suggest it is the merchants, but it is more credible to think it is one of the angels we have just met. Whoever it is, Babylon is being told that every ambition the city had is now lost, all wealth is gone and nothing that they had will ever be found again.

Verse 15: The various goods and luxuries that are itemised in verses 12 and 13, having been summed up in verse 14, were supplied by the merchants, who have now separated themselves from Babylon for fear of being caught in the judgement, and are weeping and mourning their loss from elsewhere.

Verse 16 & 17a: Everything displaying the wealth and beauty of the city will be utterly destroyed, and now they are grieving over the loss. Again emphasis is given here to the speed with which the end will come, for in one hour, it says, everything has come to nothing. Not a literal 'hour', one supposes, but at the right time and very suddenly.

Verses 17b & 18: Now we read of the shipping magnates, the commanders, the sailors, the passengers and the traders, all standing back from the destruction and watching in dismay. They all cry out, as they see the smoke and destruction, *"What is like this great city?"* They have no answer to their own question.

Verse 19: All of them throw metaphorical dust on their heads as a sign of deep mourning, and they weep over political Babylon where, from the words in this verse, their concern is more the loss of business and the source of wealth rather than the city itself.

Heaven rejoices over Babylon's destruction – verses 20 to 24

²⁰'Rejoice over her, O heaven, and you holy apostles and prophets, for God has avenged you on her!' ²¹Then a mighty angel took up a stone like a great millstone and threw it into the sea, saying, 'Thus with violence the great city Babylon shall be thrown down, and shall not be found anymore. ²²The sound of harpists, musicians, flutists, and trumpeters shall not be heard in you anymore. No craftsman of any craft shall be found in you anymore, and the sound of a millstone shall not be heard in you anymore. ²³The light of a lamp shall not shine in you anymore, and the voice of bridegroom and bride shall not be heard in you anymore. For your merchants were the great men of the earth, for by your sorcery all the nations were deceived. ²⁴And in her was found the blood of prophets and saints, and of all who were slain on the earth.'

Verse 20: John heard a voice once more, but we are not told its source. It may well have been the voice of the previous angel that spoke. Heaven, in this instance, means all those who dwell in heaven, the angelic host and the raptured saints, the apostles and the prophets. Reference to apostles and prophets raises a few questions and even more answers. It is most unlikely that this is referring here to those who today have adopted the titles 'apostles' and 'prophets', self-proclaimed and mostly without justification or calling. As is so often the case, it is better to take the literal view and to accept that these are martyred apostles and prophets, justified and holy for, as we read, God has avenged them through the destruction of both ecclesiastical and political Babylon. (Jeremiah 51:48)

Verse 21: The strength of this particular *'mighty'* angel is demonstrated by the ease with which he lifts a great stone in the form of a millstone which he throws into the sea. This is a symbolic act, one that dramatically reveals both the suddenness and the totality of political Babylon's destruction, never to be seen again. That this is speaking prophetically of a time in the future is obvious. Babylon, the original city, is still there in Mesopotamia, semi-ruined but partially and rather crudely reconstructed on Saddam Hussein's instructions. On a hill overlooking the city is a magnificent palace, built for Saddam, which could well become the Antichrist's palace of the future. The destruction that we read of in this verse will happen at the time of the Armageddon Campaign, still future, where this is confirmed in Daniel 11:44–45, verses that should be read. (Jeremiah 51:63-64)

Verse 22: As we read this verse, we can understand that three kinds of activity will cease – the life of pleasure, expressed through the musical instruments, the life of business, expressed through the reference to craft; and, finally, the life of domesticity, expressed through reference to the millstone. (Isaiah 24:8)

Verse 23: Everything will be in darkness, as no light will again be seen there; no more wedding parties will take place, for the ruins will be dead. The wealth and influence of this city had been great, but its greatness was built on sorcery and deception that entrapped the whole earth and now it's all gone. What a great contrast with the coming 'City of God'. (Jeremiah 25:10)

Verse 24: We see here that God considers Babylon, and all it represents, to be responsible for the persecution and death of the prophets and the Tribulation saints worldwide during the reign of the Antichrist. But now all trace has gone.

CHAPTER 19

The fourfold hallelujah – verses 1 to 6

¹After these things I heard a loud voice of a great multitude in heaven, saying, 'Alleluia! Salvation and glory and honour and power belong to the Lord our God! ²For true and righteous are His judgments, because He has judged the great harlot who corrupted the earth with her fornication; and He has avenged on her the blood of His servants shed by her.' ³Again they said, 'Alleluia! Her smoke rises up forever and ever!' ⁴And the twenty-four elders and the four living creatures fell down and worshipped God who sat on the throne, saying, 'Amen! Alleluia!' ⁵Then a voice came from the throne, saying, 'Praise our God, all you His servants and those who fear Him, both small and great!' ⁶And I heard, as it were, the voice of a great multitude, as the sound of many waters and as the sound of mighty thunderings, saying, 'Alleluia! For the Lord God Omnipotent reigns!'

Verse 1: The fall of mystical Babylon, the corrupt one-world church, has been completed, and therefore the destruction of the Antichrist's entire kingdom is total. In John's vision this is being celebrated in heaven, and he hears the sound of rejoicing coming from a great multitude, those who inhabit the heavenly realm, the angels surrounding the throne, the elders, the raptured saints – and probably more. This is justification for the first hallelujah for now salvation, glory and honour belong to the Lord God.

Verse 2: God is just and righteous in His judgements, for here we read He will answer the prayers of those persecuted, as we found them in chapter 6, verse 10. The great harlot has been judged and sentenced, and is no more. The one-world church, symbolised by the great harlot, corrupt, cruel and perverted, is no more. God has avenged the deaths of His servants killed by this evil church system. Do we really mean that? Yes, we do, for the precedent for severe punishment has been established through many evil acts in biblical history, but it has been much worse in the last century. But the church? Surely not! The truth is that, over centuries, the church has been responsible, directly or indirectly, for some of the worst atrocities against the Jewish people. The church? Yes, for Yeshua said this to his disciples, in Matthew 24:9:

> *'Then they will deliver you up to tribulation and kill you, and you will be hated by all nations for My name's sake.'*

This promise did not apply to the disciples and Jewish believers alone but to all believers everywhere and it will climax during the Tribulation period. (Deuteronomy 32:43)

Verse 3: Now came the second hallelujah as the smoke of the destruction of the great harlot was seen to rise, and will continue to rise forever as a memorial. While this refers to the end of mystical Babylon, it implies that the same eternal punishment will also fall upon all those who had any part in her. Political Babylon has gone, but the smoke of her burning, the legacy of her debauchery and this world's sin, will be evidenced throughout eternity. (Isaiah 34:9-10)

Verse 4: The third hallelujah came from the voices of the twenty-four elders and the *seraphim* as they confirmed the praise of the angels and the raptured saints.

Verse 5: Then there came a voice, from whom we do not know and, despite the many and varied suggestions, it is pointless to conjecture and it is best left as just a voice. It certainly wasn't from God, and not from Yeshua either, for at no time did He ever address God in the manner here. The call to the hearers, though, is to praise Him. (Psalm 22:23)

Verse 6: Now John heard a tumult of voices, a great noise a bit like standing near to the Niagara Falls, where many millions are calling out the fourth hallelujah, all because the Lord God Omnipotent has taken up His reign. (Psalm 97:1)

The Marriage of the Lamb – verses 7 to 10

[7] Let us be glad and rejoice and give Him glory, for the marriage of the Lamb has come, and His wife has made herself ready.' [8] And to her it was granted to be arrayed in fine linen, clean and bright, for the fine linen is the righteous acts of the saints. [9] Then he said to me, 'Write: "Blessed are those who are called to the marriage supper of the Lamb!"' And he said to me, 'These are the true sayings of God.' [10] And I fell at his feet to worship him. But he said to me, 'See that you do not do that! I am your fellow servant, and of your brethren who have the testimony of Jesus. Worship God! For the testimony of Jesus is the spirit of prophecy.'

Verse 7: A voice is heard speaking here but whether it is the voice of the masses of verse 6 or the unknown voice heard in verse 5 is not clear. But that doesn't matter, for it is what the voice says that is important. The destruction of Babylon is now past and we can look forward to a more wonderful prospect – the coming Marriage of the Lamb, and that really is something to rejoice about. There is one thing we can be absolutely certain of and it is that this marriage, taking place in heaven, will be based on a traditional Jewish marriage and will consist of five distinct stages:

1. The arranging of the marriage, God's plan of redemption.

2. The proposal, through Yeshua's First Coming.

3. The fetching of the bride.

4. Then there is the marriage ceremony that takes place in the home of the groom's father.

5. Finally, the marriage feast.

The first two stages have already occurred; the third will happen at the time of the Rapture, the fourth stage will take place after the Rapture, but before the Second Coming. The fifth stage will take place after the Second Coming, when Yeshua is enthroned upon earth and where there will be the great coming together of the saints of all the ages. It will be the marriage feast that will then herald in the Millennial, or Messianic kingdom, which will last for 1,000 years. Who is the bride? Again many are the views, but the most logical answer is that she is the whole body of the saints, Jews and Gentiles, both those who have died and those caught up in the Rapture, the *first resurrection*. She has made herself ready through the activity of the Holy Spirit but, in reality, it is more that Yeshua, by the giving of Himself, has brought her to a place where she has become the glorious church, holy and *without blemish and without spot* (1 Peter 1:19). As with the traditional Jewish wedding, the bride will have prepared herself through stages of purification.

Verse 8: She will be arrayed in fine linen, clean and bright, given to her by the Lord Himself. We know these garments are the symbol of righteousness and salvation, a sure sign that she is counted amongst those who have been judged, forgiven and declared justified.

Verse 9: Then we hear that someone spoke to John, but who? It is not very clear, but the general opinion is that it is one of the original seven angels of chapter 17, verse 1. John is to record that those who are invited to the marriage supper of the Lamb are greatly blessed. It was then confirmed to John that these words were from God and were the truth. We can understand this to mean, from the Jewish marriage perspective, that it is a Jewish marriage supper, or feast, to which all the friends and further relatives of the families are invited, and which occurs some period of time after the marriage ceremony. So now we have all the Old Testament saints and all the Tribulation saints, all the believers of all time, coming along to the great supper which takes place on earth after the Second Coming, and is seen symbolically in the Feast of Tabernacles. What a celebration this will be. This feast, according to the ancient rabbis was also named 'The Feast of the Final Ingathering'. How significant is that?

Verse 10: John was overwhelmed by all that he had seen and heard, and fell at the feet of this particular angel, possibly believing that this was God Himself. But the angel corrects him, saying that he and John were equals because they, with all true believers, have the testimony of Yeshua. The testimony of Yeshua is that He is the fulfilment of all prophecy, and that to find Him we need to study the words of all the prophets of the Old Testament.

The Second Coming – verses 11 to 16

[11]Now I saw heaven opened, and behold, a white horse. And He who sat on him was called Faithful and True, and in righteousness He judges and makes war. [12]His eyes were like a flame of fire, and on His head were many crowns. He had a name written that no one knew except Himself. [13]He was clothed with a robe dipped in blood, and His name is called The Word of God. [14]And the armies in heaven, clothed in fine linen, white and clean, followed Him on white horses. [15]Now out of His mouth goes a sharp sword, that with it He should strike the nations. And He Himself will rule them with a rod of iron. He Himself treads the winepress of the fierceness and wrath of Almighty God. [16]And He has on His robe and on His thigh a name written: KING OF KINGS AND LORD OF LORDS.

Verse 11: John, in this verse, must have been standing on the earth somewhere and, as he looked, he saw a gap in the heavens and in the gap he saw a white horse. Seated on the horse was none other than Yeshua, who was called '*Faithful and True*', and in righteousness He will judge and make war on His enemies. Faithful because all His promises have been there from the beginning, and now they are about to be fulfilled. They are true because, by coming as He does, He is proving Himself to be the Messiah promised of old. At this moment when John saw Him, He was appearing at the gate of the universe prior to descending to earth to bring destruction upon His enemies and defeat upon the Armageddon forces of the Antichrist. (Isaiah 11:4)

Verse 12: The description here is very vivid. Eyes like flames of fire, able to see through any obstacle, and on His head many crowns. These, in Greek, are *diadema,* crowns of kingship rather than the *stephanos* crowns of the overcomers, and they indicate His royalty and authority. He had a name written, although it doesn't say where, a name that no one but Himself could read. There has been so much conjecture over this tiny issue for, if it was intended that we should know, it would have told us.

Verse 13: He was wearing robes dipped in blood, the blood of His enemies, just as foreseen by Isaiah, in Isaiah 63:1–6, especially verses 2 and 3:

> *²Why is Your apparel red, and Your garments like one who treads in the winepress? ³'I have trodden the winepress alone, and from the peoples no one was with Me. For I have trodden them in My anger, and trampled them in My fury; their blood is sprinkled upon My garments, and I have stained all My robes.'*

His name was called the Word of God, a name used only by John, and it marks His divine nature. It is presumed not to be the name spoken of in verse 12.

Verse 14: Yeshua was followed, John now tells us, by the armies (note the plural) of heaven. So how many armies are there? It doesn't tell us, but logically there must be at least two. One of these could be the one described in Matthew 16:27, in other words an angelic army, but what about the other? We can deduce that the second army is made up of the church saints, those we call 'pre-Tribulation saints', dressed in the white linen of righteousness and riding white horses, who have experienced the Rapture and have been judged and vindicated. But turn back to Isaiah, chapter 63, for a moment, where we see that although they all return to earth with Yeshua as He comes, it is not to fight, for none join in the battle because, as it says, the battle belongs to the Lord. None wear armour, and we can therefore accept that these armies are there just to watch Yeshua's victory and to rejoice in triumph.

Verses 15: The first phrase in this verse, *'Now out of His mouth goes a sharp sword'* is a repetition of the description in chapter 1, verse 16, a sword that is the word of God, used here as a destroying weapon of judgement. It is also a symbol of Yeshua's absolute and total authority, for we are told He will rule the nations with a rod of iron, in fulfilment of the words of chapter 12, verse 5. Despite Yeshua returning with the armies of heaven following behind Him, He alone fights against the

Antichrist's forces, as we know from Isaiah 63:6, and from the words in this verse '*He Himself treads the winepress of the fierceness and wrath of Almighty God.*' The general understanding of the winepress is that it signifies the outworking of the wrath of God, and the wine flowing from it is the blood of His enemies, crushed by the feet of Him who treads the winepress. This is not real blood, of course, but is symbolic of the blood resulting from the total destruction of the Armageddon Campaign army. See how this relates to the statement in chapter 14, verse 20.

Verse 16: Yeshua's name or title was written on his clothing. Many are the views over this statement – is the name on His thigh or on His robe? Or both? Or on His crown? Does it matter? It is impossible to determine the exact location, and it's not where it is written that is important, but what is written: '*KING OF KINGS AND LORD OF LORDS.*' (Deuteronomy 10:17)

The Armageddon Campaign – verses 17 to 21

[17] *Then I saw an angel standing in the sun; and he cried with a loud voice, saying to all the birds that fly in the midst of heaven, 'Come and gather together for the supper of the great God,* [18] *that you may eat the flesh of kings, the flesh of captains, the flesh of mighty men, the flesh of horses and of those who sit on them, and the flesh of all people, free and slave, both small and great.'* [19] *And I saw the beast, the kings of the earth, and their armies, gathered together to make war against Him who sat on the horse and against His army.* [20] *Then the beast was captured, and with him the false prophet who worked signs in his presence, by which he deceived those who received the mark of the beast and those who worshipped his image. These two were cast alive into the lake of fire burning with brimstone.* [21] *And the rest were killed with the sword which proceeded from the mouth of Him who sat on the horse. And all the birds were filled with their flesh.*

Verse 17: John now saw another angel standing in the sun, a place of brightness that could be the *Shekinah*, and possibly it is the brightness surrounding the Messiah and His white horse. This angel cried out an invitation to the birds of the air. Because the coming slaughter of the armies of the nations is going to be so great, the birds are invited to the great feast of God. This is not to be confused with the coming marriage feast; it is the complete antithesis of it. (Isaiah 34:6-7)

Verse 18: It will be a feast where they will eat the flesh of the unburied carcases of men and animals, the kings and their officers, the strong men, the horses and their riders, and all those who have been part of the confederacy of the Antichrist. The events of this verse, although appearing gruesome, are merely anticipating the utter destruction of the Antichrist and his army. And it is '*the supper of the great God*' (verse 17), because He has ordained it. (Ezekiel 34:18)

Verse 19: Here in this verse we have the outcome resulting from the pouring out of the sixth bowl judgement (Revelation 16:14); the final battle of the Armageddon Campaign is about to reach its climax. The armies of the Antichrist that had gathered in the Jezreel Valley, having overcome Jerusalem, will advance against the Jewish remnant in Bozrah and against their head, Yeshua. (Joel 3:9-11)

Verse 20: They did not succeed and John saw that the Antichrist, the '*beast*', and the False Prophet, who had deceived so many such that the Antichrist was worshipped as though he was God, were captured and thrown alive into the Lake of Fire burning with brimstone. This is the '*second death*'. (Daniel 7:11)

Verse 21: From this verse we see there will be no survivors among the enemy forces, all will be destroyed, together with any of the Antichrist's followers; none will be left. The words from the mouth of Yeshua were themselves sufficient to destroy the whole army. What a magnificent description of His power. The birds of the air, whatever they represent, will have a great feast too. (Ezekiel 39:19-20)

CHAPTER 20

The Tribulation period is now past, Yeshua has returned and the forces of evil have been destroyed. Now begins a seventy-five day period in which several things happen. This period is explained in Daniel 12: 11–12:

> *¹¹And from the time that the daily sacrifice is taken away, and the abomination of desolation is set up, there shall be one thousand two hundred and ninety days. ¹² Blessed is he who waits, and comes to the one thousand three hundred and thirty-five days.*

Just what this means is not clarified by John, and it is not part of this study to speculate.

Satan bound – verses 1 to 3

> *¹Then I saw an angel coming down from heaven, having the key to the bottomless pit and a great chain in his hand. ²He laid hold of the dragon, that serpent of old, who is the Devil and Satan, and bound him for a thousand years; ³and he cast him into the bottomless pit, and shut him up, and set a seal on him, so that he should deceive the nations no more till the thousand years were finished. But after these things he must be released for a little while.*

Verse 1: Another angel appeared to John, which one it doesn't say, just an angel. In his hand he held the key to the bottomless pit, also known as the 'abyss' as we learned in chapter 1, and he also carries a strong chain.

Verse 2: Satan must have been weakened somehow by recent events, for it was just an ordinary angel that came, along with the chain and the key, not one of the celestial beings or an archangel. The angel will take Satan and bind him with the chain, and he will remain chained and banished for 1,000 years. If we look we will see that the various names given to Satan in this verse describe the many aspects of his nature, hence the need for him to be bound. (Isaiah 24:21-22)

Verse 3: The angel will then force Satan into the bottomless pit, into the lowest depths of *Sheol,* or *Hades,* before closing off the entrance and setting a seal upon it. No more will Satan be able to deceive people, not for 1,000 years, but at the end of the Millennium he will be released and will cause havoc for a brief while before facing his own destruction. We must remember that Satan was the most powerful cherub, God's 'right-hand man' at one stage, far too powerful to be challenged by an ordinary angel, but now his power has gone, Yeshua is in control, everything has changed for the good, and all Satan's authority has been stripped away.

When the Bible student considers the question of the Millennium, the word itself confronts us with a wide variety of opinions. Broadly speaking, these views fall into four categories:

No-Millennium: The expression is purely symbolic and unspecific.

Past-Millennium: The Millennium began in the fourth century with the reign of Constantine, ending in the fourteenth century with the Ottoman invasion.

Present-Millennium: Began with the First Coming and will end with the Second Coming, the time in which we now live.

Future Millennium: A period of 1,000 years, itself divided into two more opinions:

a. Post-Millennial – the Second Coming is *after* the Millennium
b. Pre–Millennial – the Second Coming is *before* the Millennium.

The final view is the only one the author considers worthy of acceptance.

The first resurrection and the Millennium – verses 4 to 6

⁴And I saw thrones, and they sat on them, and judgment was committed to them. Then I saw the souls of those who had been beheaded for their witness to Jesus and for the word of God, who had not worshiped the beast or his image, and had not received his mark on their foreheads or on their hands. And they lived and reigned with Christ for a thousand years. ⁵But the rest of the dead did not live again until the thousand years were finished. This is the first resurrection. ⁶Blessed and holy is he who has part in the first resurrection. Over such the second death has no power, but they shall be priests of God and of Christ, and shall reign with Him a thousand years.

Verse 4: John now saw thrones, almost certainly in heaven, although some say they are on earth. Without doubt they are places of great dignity and, because they were places where judgement would be dispensed, they were reserved for some very special people. But who are *'they'* at the start of this verse? Could they be the twelve apostles, who will rule over the twelve tribes of Israel? Or are they the martyrs who had not worshipped the beast? There are several other suggestions but none are, in themselves, serious enough to be considered. The preferred answer, which could be wrong, is that they are the twelve apostles (see Matthew 19:28), together with all the saints, both Old and New Testament, together with the Tribulation saints, Jew and Gentile, who will receive their reward and will live and reign with Yeshua for 1,000 years. See what Paul says, in 1 Corinthians 6:2–3:

²Do you not know that the saints will judge the world? And if the world will be judged by you, are you unworthy to judge the smallest matters? ³Do you not know that we shall judge angels? How much more, things that pertain to this life?

As part of their future role the saints will judge the world, as assessors on behalf of the Messiah, and will also judge the evil angels. (Daniel 12:2)

Verse 5: This verse appears to support the proposition of the previous verse. Bearing in mind that the raptured saints are already in heaven, it will be as the result of the Second Coming that the Tribulation saints will be raised to join them, together with the Old Testament saints, and thus they will complete the *first resurrection*. The *rest of the dead*, in other words, all unbelievers of all time who have died, will not live again until the end of the Millennium, as we shall later see. That will be the time of the final judgement and the second resurrection. (Isaiah 26:14)

Verse 6: *Blessed and holy* is something applicable to all redeemed souls but now, through the *first resurrection*, the saints move on to a higher degree of blessedness and will experience a complete and eternal consecration to God. The *second death*, which follows the second resurrection, will have no power over them. What is meant by the *second death*? It applies to all non-believers of all time, kings and commoners alike, all of whom will be raised up in the 'second resurrection' at the end of the Millennium, who will individually face judgement for thoughts, words and actions before Him who sits on the Great White Throne, and where the sentence will be eternity in the Lake of Fire. That is the *second death*. (Isaiah 26:19)

The end of Satan – verses 7 to 10

⁷Now when the thousand years have expired, Satan will be released from his prison ⁸and will go out to deceive the nations which are in the four corners of the earth, Gog and Magog, to gather them together to battle, whose number is as the sand of the sea. ⁹They went up on the breadth of the earth and surrounded the camp of the saints and the beloved city. And fire came down from God out of heaven and devoured them. ¹⁰The devil, who deceived them, was cast into the lake of fire and brimstone where the beast and the false prophet are. And they will be tormented day and night forever and ever.

Verse 7: The release of Satan from his incarceration in the bottomless pit will be the signal that the Millennium, the 1,000-year period, is over. That he is released at all is because of God's divine plan for testing both him and the entire population still living on the earth.

Verse 8: He will celebrate his release by setting out on his favourite pastime of deception. A thousand years have passed since his imprisonment, and by this time there will be many people populating the earth, those nations that were left in the world at the start of the Millennium and have multiplied since. Satan will set out to deceive them into making another attempt to destroy God's people. His intention is to build a huge army, calling on men from the four corners of the earth, meaning everywhere, and named here as Gog and Magog, with the intention of completing what the Gog of Magog war of Ezekiel 38 and 39 failed to achieve – the destruction of Israel. The earlier war, according to prophecy, will occur prior to the Tribulation period and will result in the total annihilation of the Gog of Magog forces through divine intervention. Apart from the name, there is no connection whatever between the war recorded by Ezekiel and this one that John foresees; they are totally distinct. But now, despite the memory of that crushing defeat many years earlier, Satan will try again, and will succeed in gathering together a huge army, without number. (Ezekiel 38:2).

Verse 9: This army will then advance to surround the camp of the saints, those believers who have mobilised to defend the *'beloved city'*, Jerusalem. In just one short sentence it tells us that God will send fire from heaven that will devour the enemy; there will be nothing left. It is interesting to note the opinions of many commentators who take the extraordinary view that the *'beloved city'* is an expression describing the Christian church, but such an interpretation would be ignoring the context. It is, of course, the earthly Jerusalem, and not the new one. That is yet to come. (Deuteronomy 23:14)

Verse 10: After this stunning defeat, the devil, Satan, will be thrown into the lake of fire and brimstone, where he will join the Antichrist and the False Prophet already in the place where they, and those who have rejected the Messiah, all those whose names are not in the Lamb's Book of Life, will endure the flames for ever and ever. Those teaching that death means annihilation, that eternal judgement is nonsense and God, if He exists at all, is a God of mercy and love, are in for a nasty surprise. He's far more than that.

The Great White Throne Judgement
and the second death –
verses 11 to 15

[11] Then I saw a great white throne and Him who sat on it, from whose face the earth and the heaven fled away. And there was found no place for them. [12] And I saw the dead, small and great, standing before God,[a] and books were opened. And another book was opened, which is the Book of Life. And the dead were judged according to their works, by the things which were written in the books. [13] The sea gave up the dead who were in it, and Death and Hades delivered up the dead who were in them. And they were judged, each one according to his works. [14] Then Death and Hades were cast into the lake of fire. This is the second death.[b] [15] And anyone not found written in the Book of Life was cast into the lake of fire.

Verse 11: John now saw a Great White Throne, white because it is the symbol of the holiness and purity of the One seated on it. Although not named, the One seated on the throne is almost certainly Yeshua the Messiah, because all judgement had been given to Him. This is confirmed in John 5:22:

> *For the Father judges no one, but has committed all judgment to the Son ...*

The earth and heavens fled away, even as John was looking, and they ceased to exist, but at what stage we are not sure, nor do we have any indication where John was looking from, but we must remember this is all visionary. This passing away of all things corruptible, however, is real and was forecast in 2 Peter 3:10–12:

> *[10] But the day of the Lord will come as a thief in the night, in which the heavens will pass away with a great noise, and the elements will melt with fervent heat; both the earth and the works that are in it will be burned up. [11] Therefore, since all these things will be dissolved, what manner of persons ought you to be in holy conduct and godliness, [12] looking for and hastening the coming of the day of God, because of which the heavens will be dissolved, being on fire, and the elements will melt with fervent heat?*

Verse 12: John, at that moment, then had a view of the dead of all time, as in verse 5, in what form we don't know, but presumably recognisable as human beings. There were huge numbers of them, made up the wicked of all ages, from Adam on. All those not included in the *first resurrection* will be there, together with all those who die during the Millennium and those still alive at its close. There is no indication of any intermediate resurrections, as some say. In 2 Corinthians 5:10, Paul says:

> For we must all appear before the judgment seat of Christ, that each one may receive the things done in the body, according to what he has done, whether good or bad.

On the basis of this verse, we can accept that everyone will be judged, except those who were in heaven who will have been judged already, but now, before the Great White Throne, not only the dead but all those alive at this time will also be judged, some for their sins deserving punishment, others for their righteousness and deserving reward. As can be imagined, the words *'and books were opened. And another book was opened'*, etc., have caused much debate. The most logical answer to this conundrum is that there are three books. The first book records the birth of every living human being. The second book records the lives, words and works of every individual ever born, in what is called *'the Book of Life'*. Depending on the details found in this book, at the time of judgement, individual names will be copied into, and recorded in, the Lamb's Book of Life, or they will not. The names of those who have experienced spiritual rebirth will then be found in the Lamb's Book of Life, but those that are not face eternity in the Lake of Fire. (Psalm 62:12).

Verse 13: Here is confirmation of the second resurrection as the dead, all of them of all time, with the exception of those of the first resurrection mentioned earlier, all those who died at sea or are buried in the ground will be raised to life to stand before the Great White Throne where, as we read in the previous verse, they will be judged according to their lives and works.

Verse 14: The good news that John then imparts is that death and hell are also cast into the Lake of Fire, and that this Lake is the destination for all those condemned to the *'second death'*. For those whose names are found in the Lamb's Book of Life this is good news, for we learn that hell will cease to exist and that there will be no more death.

Verse 15: The important thing for us all to realise is that when we come to this particular stage in history, every person ever born will, through belief in Yeshua, spend eternity in the Eternal Kingdom with Yeshua, but those who have rejected Him will spend eternity in the Lake of Fire. Death, therefore, is not the end of life, as some mistakenly believe. Unfortunately, John does not make particular reference here to those living at the end of the Millennium and who will be declared righteous, but we can safely assume that they will continue to live on into the Eternal Kingdom, as can be determined from verses 24 to 27 of the next chapter, where they will have a place of security with Yeshua. (Psalm 69:28)

CHAPTER 21

A new heaven and a new earth – verses 1 to 8

¹Now I saw a new heaven and a new earth, for the first heaven and the first earth had passed away. Also there was no more sea. ²Then I, John, saw the holy city, New Jerusalem, coming down out of heaven from God, prepared as a bride adorned for her husband. ³And I heard a loud voice from heaven saying, 'Behold, the tabernacle of God is with men, and He will dwell with them, and they shall be His people. God Himself will be with them and be their God. ⁴And God will wipe away every tear from their eyes; there shall be no more death, nor sorrow, nor crying. There shall be no more pain, for the former things have passed away.' ⁵Then He who sat on the throne said, 'Behold, I make all things new.' And He said to me, 'Write, for these words are true and faithful.' ⁶And He said to me, 'It is done! I am the Alpha and the Omega, the Beginning and the End. I will give of the fountain of the water of life freely to him who thirsts. ⁷He who overcomes shall inherit all things, and I will be his God and he shall be My son. ⁸But the cowardly, unbelieving, abominable, murderers, sexually immoral, sorcerers, idolaters, and all liars shall have their part in the lake which burns with fire and brimstone, which is the second death.'

Verse 1: John now saw something wonderful, the revelation concerning the eternal state of the earth and the heavens. The earth, as we know it today, will have been in a state of disrepair following the Tribulation period, virtually wrecked, but renovated for the Millennial Age so that it can be inhabited again by the survivors. But now the old order has been done away with, nothing of the old order of earth and heaven remains and a completely new order, the Eternal Order, with a brand-new earth and heavens is just beginning.

One major change that will be noticed is that there will be no more sea. It is debatable whether this means the oceans will be no more, since it was from the sea that the beast came, a bit of a disappointment for those who like a day at the seaside, or that the turbulent sea, where that speaks of wicked nations, will cease to be. There is no clear consensus on this. (Isaiah 65:17; Isaiah 66:22)

Verse 2: Next, John saw the Holy City, the New Jerusalem, coming down from heaven. As far as the new earth and the new heavens are concerned, God will create everything afresh. But note that He doesn't create a New Jerusalem, and that's because the Holy City has been waiting in the third heaven from the beginning of time, and when the new earth has been prepared and all is ready, it will come to be established on the earth, in the new Israel. This New Jerusalem, made ready as a bride for her husband, is really the sum of perfected humanity, all the saints of the Rapture, all in total unity, and it is these who are the bride of the Messiah.

Verse 3: John now heard a great voice, probably not from God but from one of the many angels, saying that the tabernacle, the dwelling place of God, will now be with men, thus fulfilling Leviticus 26:11–12:

> *I will set My tabernacle among you, and My soul shall not abhor you.*
> *I will walk among you and be your God, and you shall be My people.*

God says in this verse that He will dwell among men and women and they will be His people, for He will be among them and will be their God. But it will not be God alone who will dwell in the Holy City, it will also be the home of the angels and the saints, Jews and Gentiles alike. (Ezekiel 37:27-28)

Verse 4: Not only will God gently wipe away tears from the eyes of those who have suffered hardship and loss, even death through the ages and at the hands of the Antichrist's forces, but He will also create things so that no more tears will ever be shed again. The old systems have gone, never to be replaced. No more pain, no more torture, no more death, for all of that is now past and will be no more. (Isaiah 25:8)

Verse 5: John then heard from the One sitting on the throne, where we assume this is still the Great White Throne, saying: *'Behold, I make all things new.'* The state that existed before, where sin and death were to be found, will be changed, and the change will apply to everything. The speaker then speaks directly to John, saying that he should record all that he has seen and heard, because everything could be relied upon as absolute truth. This is important to us as believers, because we need a sound basis for our belief and, because every event recorded in this book will happen and, as we see them unfold, those of us still here shall have confidence for the ultimate fulfilment of every promise.

Verse 6: Who the One is sitting on the throne, whether it is God or Yeshua, does not concern us, for they are one and the same. He spoke to John telling him that all was done, it was finished. This phrase echoes the words of Yeshua when He was on the cross, and when He died, God's perfect plan for the redemption of men was complete. Now His plan of judgement and wrath is also finished and complete, and His intentions for the restoration of His special people, Israel, will be fulfilled. He was before all things, from whom all things created grew and developed, and He is at the end of all things, where all things converge to His glory. From this time on, for anyone who thirsts, there will be fountains of living water, meaning that the waters of life will be available at all times for those who seek to drink. The thirst spoken of here is not natural thirst but is the thirst of one seeking Yeshua and the salvation obtained through Him. The benefits of 'drinking' are pardon for sin, righteousness and justification for, as we drink, we take Yeshua into our being and conform to His likeness. The water, therefore, symbolises God's grace, abundant and free.

Verse 7: And now, in this verse, we read of the complete and total fulfilment of all God's promises, as we found them in chapter 2, verse 26, where the overcomer, that's all those who are the residents of the new earth, will now inherit all things – the glorious New Jerusalem, the new creation, no more sorrow, no more death, and the fullness and freeness of the waters of life. Not only that but the overcomer will dwell with and know the living God.

Verse 8: These wonderful promises are followed in this verse by another promise which is much less pleasant. All those listed in this verse are in sharp contrast to the overcomers, for here are all those who, by nature of their sinfulness, are apostates with no right of access to heaven. Their rightful place, their only place now, is the Lake of Fire, which burns continuously and this, for them, is the second death.

The bride of the Lamb: The New Jerusalem – verses 9 to 27

⁹Then one of the seven angels who had the seven bowls filled with the seven last plagues came to me and talked with me, saying, 'Come, I will show you the bride, the Lamb's wife.' ¹⁰And he carried me away in the Spirit to a great and high mountain, and showed me the great city, the holy Jerusalem, descending out of heaven from God, ¹¹having the glory of God. Her light was like a most precious stone, like a jasper stone, clear as crystal. ¹²Also she had a great and high wall with twelve gates, and twelve angels at the gates, and names written on them, which are the names of the twelve tribes of the children of Israel: ¹³three gates on the east, three gates on the north, three gates on the south, and three gates on the west. ¹⁴Now the wall of the city had twelve foundations, and on them were the names of the twelve apostles of the Lamb. ¹⁵And he who talked with me had a gold reed to measure the city, its gates, and its wall. ¹⁶The city is laid out as a square; its length is as great as its breadth. And he measured the city with the reed: twelve thousand furlongs. Its length, breadth, and height are equal. ¹⁷Then he measured its wall: one hundred and forty-four cubits, according to the measure of a man, that is, of an angel. ¹⁸The construction of its wall was of jasper; and the city was pure gold, like clear glass. ¹⁹The foundations of the wall of the city were adorned with all kinds of precious stones: the first foundation was jasper, the second sapphire, the third chalcedony, the fourth emerald, ²⁰the fifth sardonyx, the sixth sardius, the seventh chrysolite, the eighth beryl, the ninth topaz, the tenth chrysoprase, the eleventh jacinth, and the twelfth amethyst. ²¹The twelve gates were twelve pearls: each individual gate was of one pearl. And the street of the city was pure gold, like transparent glass. ²²But I saw no temple in it, for the Lord God Almighty and the Lamb are its temple. ²³The city had no need of the sun or of the moon to shine in it, for the glory of God illuminated it. The Lamb is its light. ²⁴And the nations of those who are saved shall walk in its light, and the kings of the earth bring their glory and honour into it. ²⁵Its gates shall not be shut at all by day (there shall be no night there). ²⁶And they shall bring the glory and the honour of the nations into it. ²⁷But there shall by no means enter it anything that defiles, or causes an abomination or a lie, but only those who are written in the Lamb's Book of Life.

Verse 9: One of the seven angels, one of those who had poured out the bowl judgements, then came to John, probably the one who showed him the great harlot in chapter 17, verse 1. Note the contrast here, because he is now going to take John to a place where he will be able to see the coming of the bride, the Lamb's wife.

Verse 10: There is here a repetition of chapter 17, verse 3, as John is taken *'in the Spirit'* to a high mountain where he is shown the great city, the New Jerusalem, coming down from God in heaven. John is here taken to a privileged place where he can get the best view of this wonderful vision, first revealed to him in verse 2 of this chapter. To attempt to spiritualise this vision would be contrary to the prophetic understanding we have discovered in this book. If we are to identify with what is being described here, we need to accept it as it is written. (Ezekiel 40:2)

Verse 11: John does his best here to describe what he was seeing, brilliance like the reflection of sunlight on many lustrous jewels as if they were diamonds. The New Jerusalem was not spotlighted as if from a distance, but was illuminated from within by the *Shekinah*, the glory of the presence of God Himself, shining like diamonds.

Verse 12: The city had a great high wall surrounding it, thus indicating its total protection and security. And it had twelve gates; at each gate there was an angel stationed, not to guard it, because there are now no enemies to guard against, but to show the ordered nature of the city. There were names written on each gate – the names of the twelve tribes of Israel. This tells us that the names of the twelve tribes will be remembered through all eternity. (Ezekiel 48:31-34)

Verse 13: Although no dimensions are given here, we can deduce that the city was in the form of a square, having three gates in each of the four sides, equally divided, and all assumed open.

Verse 14: The four walls, built on twelve foundation stones, have led to some speculation. Are the foundations twelve separate stones, perhaps, or are they twelve layers, each built one upon another and running all round under the four sides? This we cannot tell, but what is clear is that on these foundations were the names of the twelve apostles, where these, too, will be remembered for all eternity.

Verse 15: The angel speaking with John is seen as having a golden measuring rod, the purpose of which was that he could measure the city, its walls and its gates. The meaning here is that John was being shown that the city was not some imaginary thing but would, when it came, be absolutely real. (Ezekiel 40:3-5)

Verse 16: We cannot be adamant about the dimension given here, 12,000 furlongs, or 1,500 miles, but it is clearly stated that this is the length of each side of a square and of its height. Taken literally, as it should be, the city will be a cube in shape. There may be something in the translation that might confuse things, for the furlong is neither a Hebrew nor a Greek measure. The general feeling is that such dimensions, right or wrong, cannot be imagined, and are probably intended as symbolic of the grandeur and symmetry of the city.

Verse 17: Now we are given another measurement, the wall is 144 cubits, but we are not told if this is height or thickness, or both. In some ways this contradicts the measurement given in the previous verse, suggesting that the symbolic view is the right one. It tells us the measurements are in cubits, the measure of a man and an angel; this must surely mean that the angel used man's measures, where 144 cubits is about the same as 220 feet Imperial.

Verse 18: John now describes the composition of the city. The wall, he says, was of jasper, a shade of green, while the city was of transparent gold.

Verses 19 & 20: As for the foundations of the city walls, these were decorated with all kinds of precious stones: the first was jasper, the second sapphire, the third chalcedony, the fourth emerald, the fifth sardonyx, the sixth sardius, the seventh chrysolite, the eighth beryl, the ninth topaz, the tenth chrysoprase, the eleventh jacinth, and the twelfth amethyst. An amazing sight. (Isaiah 54:11-12)

Verse 21: We now learn that the twelve gates are each made from one pearl which, altogether, reveal a picture of great and awesome glory where our human minds struggle to even imagine the appearance.

Verse 22: John noticed, however, that there was no temple in the city, and the reason for this, he says, is that a temple will be redundant, for it is the Lord God and the Lamb that, in themselves, are the temple. This surely means that both God Himself and His Messiah will be visible and accessible at all times to everyone.

Verse 23: Other omissions in the New Jerusalem are the sun and the moon that will no longer be needed. That's because God and the Lamb being everywhere are always surrounded by the radiance of the *Shekinah*, which has a glory brighter than the sun and the moon. (Isaiah 60:19-20)

Verse 24: The understanding of this verse is that as we have now moved into the Eternal Kingdom, there will be no other inhabitants of the new earth beyond the saints of all time who are the New Jerusalem, as we learned in verse 2 of this chapter. They will be joined by all the righteous of all the nations who have lived through the Millennium and who will live in the light of God's glory. All those among the saved who once held positions of power and authority in the millennial order, kings and princes and prime ministers, will bring their own glory into the city in submission to God and to the Lamb. And so it will be that the final consummation of God's purposes and plans are now completed. (Isaiah 60:3-5)

Verse 25: The gates will never be closed because it will always be day and there is no enemy outside. (Isaiah 60:11)

Verse 26: Any glory belonging to any nation, and the honour attached to it, will be brought into the city. (Isaiah 60:16)

Verse 27: The only qualification for anyone to enter the New City will be that their names are written in the Lamb's Book of Life. Just as sin was expelled from the Garden of Eden, so shall nothing corrupted by Satan be permitted to enter in, no temptation to sin, the stain of earthly corruption will have no place. (Isaiah 52:1)

CHAPTER 22

The river and the tree of life – verses 1 to 5

¹And he showed me a pure river of water of life, clear as crystal, proceeding from the throne of God and of the Lamb. ²In the middle of its street, and on either side of the river, was the tree of life, which bore twelve fruits, each tree yielding its fruit every month. The leaves of the tree were for the healing of the nations. ³And there shall be no more curse, but the throne of God and of the Lamb shall be in it, and His servants shall serve Him. ⁴They shall see His face, and His name shall be on their foreheads. ⁵There shall be no night there: They need no lamp nor light of the sun, for the Lord God gives them light. And they shall reign forever and ever.

Verse 1: John is next shown, presumably by the angel of the previous chapter, a river which flows from the throne of God. Just how that can be is another of those unexplained mysteries, but something we do learn is that it is a river of pure water, crystal clear. Some say that what we have here must surely be considered as something symbolic, where the waters are really those of peace and spiritual life and those drinking of them are immortal, never to die. However, in Ezekiel 47:1–12, we read of water flowing out from the Millennial temple, and we may therefore see this as an uninterrupted flow of life for the benefit of the saints, ever fresh, coming from the fountainhead of grace, the throne of the Father and the Son. Note that there is only one throne, which surely implies the unity of God the Father and Yeshua the Lamb. It shows both the equal dignity of their persons and the equality of their love for mankind, the citizens of the New Jerusalem. (Ezekiel 47:1)

Verse 2: This is one verse that really tests our imaginations. According to the majority of the experts, the best understanding we can have is to think of the river as flowing through a broad street, but that doesn't help a great deal. In Genesis 2 we read of the tree of life, which appeared first in the Garden of Eden, and is now back in its place. Its trunk, which spans the river to both sides, supports the tree, which is very productive, yielding a different crop of fruits every month. There is some dispute as to whether twelve different kinds of fruit are intended, or whether it means twelve crops of the same kind. The latter suggestion is to be preferred because of the words '*each tree yielding its fruit every month*'. But then we have the words '*each* tree' which gives the impression that there is more than one tree, possible twelve, although few translations are rendered in this way. There is no answer to questions like, what is the fruit for? And what about the leaves? We have just been told that sickness, pain and death are gone for ever, so why are leaves needed for healing? The answer may be in the translation. The Greek word for 'healing', in this verse, is *thĕrapĕia*, from which we get therapeutic, which may give the meaning as 'to maintain health'. Another, possibly more accurate translation from the Greek, is '*service rendered by one to another*', but that doesn't help much. We must wait for the answer. (Ezekiel 47:12)

Verse 3: In this verse the key word is 'curse'. Why should the thought of 'curses' arise in the perfect state of the Eternal Order? It might be that the more accurate translation of the Greek word for 'curse' used here, '*katanathema*', with the meaning 'imprecate', which means to invoke a response, would seem to suggest that there is nothing more that deserves God's curse. That, it seems, is because the throne of God and the Lamb is in the midst of the people, and it is there that God's servants will serve Him through their priestly functions for ever. (Zechariah 14:11)

Verse 4: His servants shall have free access into His immediate presence, an honour not experienced by any before this time, and seldom available for ordinary individuals to meet their earthly sovereigns. It is the reward for those who are pure in heart. The phrase *'His name shall be on their foreheads'* implies total consecration to the service of God, and is unlikely to be some visible mark. (Psalm 17:15)

Verse 5: Just as we learned that the gates of the city would never be closed so there is the understanding that it will be continuous day, there will be no interruptions for rest or sleep, and joyful service will be continuous. And there will be no need for lamps or light from the sun for God will give them light, as it says in chapter 21, verse 23. They will reign for ever and ever, in a higher sense than reigning in the Millennium, but over what? It is suggested that it could mean reigning over parts of the universe of God's creation, but we cannot be sure. (Zechariah 14:7)

Verse 5 brings us to the end of the apocalyptic element of the Book of Revelation. We have learned pretty well all we can about the New Jerusalem. It tells us little about what people will do when they get there, but in this state they shall reign with Yeshua for a thousand years, and continue to reign continuously in the Eternal Kingdom. Just what that means for us – we shall obviously have to wait and see!

Conclusion and benediction – verses 6 to 21

⁶Then he said to me, 'These words are faithful and true.' And the Lord God of the holy prophets sent His angel to show His servants the things which must shortly take place. ⁷'Behold, I am coming quickly! Blessed is he who keeps the words of the prophecy of this book.' ⁸Now I, John, saw and heard these things. And when I heard and saw, I fell down to worship before the feet of the angel who showed me these things. ⁹Then he said to me, 'See that you do not do that. For I am your fellow servant, and of your brethren the prophets, and of those who keep the words of this book. Worship God.' ¹⁰And he said to me, 'Do not seal the words of the prophecy of this book, for the time is at hand. ¹¹He who is unjust, let him be unjust still; he who is filthy, let him be filthy still; he who is righteous, let him be righteous still; he who is holy, let him be holy still. ¹²And behold, I am coming quickly, and My reward is with Me, to give to every one according to his work. ¹³I am the Alpha and the Omega, the Beginning and the End, the First and the Last.' ¹⁴Blessed are those who do His commandments, that they may have the right to the tree of life, and may enter through the gates into the city. [15]But outside are dogs and sorcerers and sexually immoral and murderers and idolaters, and whoever loves and practices a lie. [16]'I, Jesus, have sent My angel to testify to you these things in the churches. I am the Root and the Offspring of David, the Bright and Morning Star.' [17]And the Spirit and the bride say, 'Come!' And let him who hears say, 'Come!' And let him who thirsts come. Whoever desires, let him take the water of life freely. [18]For I testify to everyone who hears the words of the prophecy of this book: If anyone adds to these things, God will add to him the plagues that are written in this book; [19]and if anyone takes away from the words of the book of this prophecy, God shall take away his part from the Book of Life, from the holy city, and from the things which are written in this book. [20]He who testifies to these things says, 'Surely I am coming quickly.' Amen. Even so, come, Lord Jesus! [21]The grace of our Lord Jesus Christ be with you all. Amen.

Verse 6: Again John heard a voice, but there is no indication of who is speaking. The general opinion is that it was the angel of chapter 21, verse 9, but it could have been any angel, or Yeshua, or even God Himself. *'These words are faithful and true'* is speaking of the testimony John has received and confirms that every word is trustworthy and true. It was God who inspired the prophets of old by His Spirit, communicating with them directly or through angels, and now, He says, everything that they prophesied *'must shortly take place'*.

Verse 7: The words *'Behold, I am coming quickly!'* appear to be spoken by the angel, but are surely on behalf of Yeshua, although there are some who think it was Yeshua Himself, probably correctly. They declare that when He does come, His appearance will be sudden, no prior warning. Again we see that the purpose of prophecy is to show us, God's servants, what is to come, that we may be ready, watching and wakeful. We are to be blessed if we keep the words of this book, even if we don't fully know and understand them. Look back to chapter 1, verse 3.

Verse 8: That John has seen and heard all that has been revealed to him confirms the authenticity of this book. No doubt the emotions he felt overwhelmed him, emotions of awe, adoration and gratitude, and it was this that caused him to fall on his face before the angelic messenger.

Verse 9: But John was told not to place angels too highly and in the wrong position, for they were fellow servants, having a different role. It is God alone who is to be worshipped.

Verse 10: The contents of this book are not to be sealed, unlike the instructions given to Daniel. If we do not get help with Daniel's prophecy relating to this time it means it will not be understood by many – but now, with the Book of Revelation, we have the key to Daniel's writings; therefore the book can be open, and kept open, for all to read and understand. Why do we need to understand the contents? It's because the times spoken of really are close at hand. (Daniel 12:9)

Verse 11: However, injustice and unrighteousness will continue in this world for a time, and this book will not change that; the unjust will continue to be unjust and the unrighteous will continue to be unrighteous through their ungodly acts. But the righteous will practise righteousness, and the holy will practise holiness. (Daniel 12:10)

Verse 12: Here again are the words speaking of Yeshua's imminent return. In this instance it is He who is speaking, where He explains the purpose for His return through the Second Coming – it is to bring His rewards. Everyone to be judged before the Great White Throne will be judged according to what he or she has done. There will be eternal punishment for the unrighteous, but justice and crowns for the righteous. (Isaiah 40:10)

Verse 13: In this verse, Yeshua was clearly stating who He is, and establishes His absolute authority. He is in control of eternity, and everything He has said will come to pass. (Isaiah 44:6)

Verse 14: Here we have a description of those who will inhabit the New Jerusalem, the Holy City. They will be obedient (in the ASV it says *'that wash their robes'*), by which we mean righteous, those who are clothed in the white robes of salvation, and they will have the right to partake of the tree of life – never to die. (Genesis 3:22-24)

Verse 15: In contrast, we now have a description of those who will not get in, the unsaved – it doesn't matter how nice or good they may have been, if they have practised magic, immorality, committed murder, idolatry and falsehood, and have not accepted the saving gospel of Yeshua, they will not get in, and will carry the characteristics of their unrighteousness throughout all eternity in the Lake of Fire. Obviously the 'dogs' mentioned are not of the canine variety, but are representing corrupt humanity. (Deuteronomy 23:18)

Verse 16: In this verse we have the only affirmation that it is Yeshua Himself who is here speaking audibly with John. It is He who has sent His angelic messengers. He confirms His character when He says He is the *'Root and the Offspring of David'* which defines His earthly heritage, while the *'Bright and Morning Star'* defines His heavenly nature.

Verse 17: Here we have the invitation that is extended to all, to accept the free gift of salvation. It is the Holy Spirit and the bride, the redeemed church, together, that have the responsibility for communicating the message – not separating the visible from the invisible, but in unity. How does that work? Simply that it is the responsibility of the church to present the whole gospel while, at the same time, the Holy Spirit does the convicting. This is the last and final invitation, still open, that is given to those who are weary and heavy-laden, and desire to drink of the waters of life. Come, drink, it's free!

Verses 18 & 19: In these two verses, we have warnings that are not adequately heeded by many today. The first is against making any additions to the word, or to preach any false and irrelevant interpretations of it, because those that do will experience all the plagues of the book – in other words, they will experience all the horrors of the Great Tribulation and will end up in the Lake of Fire. Not only is this warning directed at apostate Christianity, but it is also addressed to the cults and false religions, where one basic commonality is that each has its own book that it rates as equal, or even superior, to the Holy Scriptures. For all of these there is no salvation, it is hidden from them, and their destination, too, will be the Lake of Fire. Likewise, any who diminish the word, denying any part of it, will lose any place in the Book of Life, will have no access to the Holy City, and will miss out on the many promises – and we know what that means. (Deuteronomy 4:2, 12:32)

Verse 20: Here, in this verse, we have another affirmation – and because it is the testimony of Yeshua, we can guarantee the truthfulness of this revelation. We also have another consideration – the swift and sudden return of Yeshua the Messiah, at any time, known only to the Father. When He does come, it will be to fulfil all prophecy, so we need to take careful heed of all that has been written.

Verse 21: Finally, we have a benediction, the appropriate end to all that we have been considering. Just as this book began with a benediction so, appropriately, it ends with one.

About the Author

Edward Thomas spent his working life in electrical engineering. On retirement, he and his wife moved to Cumbria, to the much-loved Lake District. In the 1970s, an incident brought Israel to the forefront of his thinking, and he began to research the scriptures to find the truth. He knew the Lord's calling to be associated with Ellel Ministries in 1993, and served with them for fourteen years as a counsellor and teacher. His heart is in communicating the truth of God's purposes for both Israel and the church, explaining it in a clear and simple way.

Lightning Source UK Ltd.
Milton Keynes UK
UKOW02f0903080916

282512UK00002B/66/P